G04AMM9.13

All About Network Directories

All About Network Directories

**Understanding Directory Services
and Business Applications**

Kevin Kampman
and
Christina Kampman

Wiley Computer Publishing

John Wiley & Sons, Inc.
NEW YORK · CHICHESTER · WEINHEIM · BRISBANE · SINGAPORE · TORONTO

658.0557
K15a

Publisher: Robert Ipsen
Editor: Carol A. Long
Managing Editor: Marnie Wielage
Text Design & Composition: Carlisle Communications

Designations used by companies to distinguish their products are often claimed as trademarks. In all instances where John Wiley & Sons, Inc., is aware of a claim, the product names appear in initial capital or ALL CAPITAL LETTERS. Readers, however, should contact the appropriate companies for more complete information regarding trademarks and registration.

This book is printed on acid-free paper.

Copyright © 2000 by Kevin Kampman and Christina Kampman. All rights reserved.

Published by John Wiley & Sons, Inc.

Published simultaneously in Canada.

No part of this publication may be reproduced, stored in a retrieval system or transmitted in any form or by any means, electronic, mechanical, photocopying, recording, scanning or otherwise, except as permitted under Sections 107 or 108 of the 1976 United States Copyright Act, without either the prior written permission of the Publisher, or authorization through payment of the appropriate per-copy fee to the Copyright Clearance Center, 222 Rosewood Drive, Danvers, MA 01923, (978) 750-8400, fax (978) 750-4744. Requests to the Publisher for permission should be addressed to the Permissions Department, John Wiley & Sons, Inc., 605 Third Avenue, New York, NY 10158-0012, (212) 850-6011, fax (212) 850-6008, E-Mail: PERMREQ@WILEY.COM.

This publication is designed to provide accurate and authoritative information in regard to the subject matter covered. It is sold with the understanding that the publisher is not engaged in professional services. If professional advice or other expert assistance is required, the services of a competent professional person should be sought.

Library of Congress Cataloging-in-Publication Data:
Kampman, Kevin, 1954-
    All about network directories : understanding directory services and business applications / Kevin Kampman, Christina Kampman.
      p. cm.
    "Wiley computer publishing."
    Includes index.
    ISBN 0-471-33363-8 (paper)
    1. Electronic directories. 2. Directories. I. Kampman, Christina, 1952- II. Title.
HE8721.K36 2000
658'.05571376—dc21   99-088937

Printed in the United States of America.

10 9 8 7 6 5 4 3 2 1

For Christopher and Jeffrey.
Paradise itself is dim, and joyless,
if not shared with them!

University Libraries
Carnegie Mellon University
Pittsburgh, PA 15213-3890

Contents

Acknowledgments

Without the help and support of Dan Blum, Dave Kosiur, Jamie Lewis, Carol Long, and Christina Berry, this book would not have been possible.

Family and friends were invaluable sources of moral support, especially the Mangios, the Kampmans, and the Shawnee Springs gang. Thank you all!

Introduction

Overview of the Book and Technology

We live in a networked world. It is hard to imagine not being able to pick up a telephone and call someone, whenever we want, from wherever we are. With the ever-increasing use of satellite and cellular technologies, people can reach each other at almost every point on the globe.

The growth of the Internet and the widespread use of networking technologies are quickly building the same expectations about computer communications from home and work. As user expectations for expanded access grow, the number of resources associated with networked communications has also grown rapidly. To accommodate this growth, mechanisms for locating resources are being expanded to provide sufficient address space for multiple devices on every square foot of the planet.

As our need to communicate with others grows, our ability to communicate with them using the post office, the telephone, or the Web is aided or hindered by our ability to locate the resources and people with whom we want to communicate. If you are trying to locate someone, you have access to a wealth of information to help you in your search. Telephone services, for example, can locate people around the country or around the world. Database services, commercial publishers, government agencies, and associations all publish tools to help you locate the people you wish to talk to. As the need to manage information associated with networked computing grows, integrated network management tools assist users when they try to locate other people on the network or the resources available to them. The lists and data sources about people and resources are known as *directories*.

With this proliferation of information, the manner in which information about people and resources is stored and accessed is undergoing a revolution. First, standards bodies and the software development community are addressing standards for publishing and finding the information. Second, the nature and kinds of information being published are changing to facilitate industry and commerce. Directories are quickly becoming the method of choice for accessing information and resources in diverse and complicated organizations.

The focus of this book is how organizations collect, manage, and publish information about people and resources in a networked computing environment. The book is intended to give you an overview of directories and directory technologies, standards, planning and managing directories in your organization, and future issues in directory implementation.

Who Should Read This Book

This book is aimed at business and IT managers, network managers, and anyone involved with networked computer installations who needs an introduction to directories and their application. Because the book is intended to be an overview of the subject, we assume that you have some knowledge of basic networking principles but otherwise have had no exposure to directories. Our goal is to provide you with enough background so that you can understand the concepts, standards, operating environment, and implementation issues associated with directories.

This book starts with an introduction to the basic concepts that form the foundation of your understanding of directories. We then discuss how directories are used in a wide variety of operating systems, applications, and network management tools. We devote a chapter to directory planning issues and a chapter to the emerging technology known as meta-directories, and we then discuss future trends in the final chapter of the book. If you have no previous experience with directories, you will want to read Chapters 1 through 3 in their entirety and then select the chapters in the rest of the book that match your interest. If you have a good grasp of the basic terminology, standards, and structure of directories, you will want to skim quickly through Chapters 1 through 3. You too can then select the chapters of major concern to you from the remainder of the book.

How This Book Is Organized

This book consists of 12 chapters. Chapters 1–3 present basic information about directories and directory services, and the standards associated with them. Chapter 4 discusses planning for directory implementation. Chapters 5–7 are an overview of the applications for directories. Chapters 8 and 9 provide a detailed review of the role of directories in the offerings of major vendors of network operating systems and applications. Chapter 10 discusses the role of the directory in telephony and video conferencing. Chapter 11 presents information about meta-directories, and Chapter 12 looks to the future. The following paragraphs give you more information about the contents of each chapter.

Chapter 1, "Directories and Their Importance to the Enterprise," gives an overview of the concepts and terminology associated with directories, talks about the problems directories are intended to solve, and presents the role of directories in a business setting.

Chapter 2, "Standards," identifies the major organizations involved in the production and maintenance of the standards essential to directories and directory services. We describe the two major directory-related standards, X.500 and LDAP, in detail.

Chapter 3, "Directory Basics," focuses on the information stored in the directory and the components that make up a directory system. These components include technical specifications, the information architecture, application program interfaces, and management tools. We provide a definition of each and a detailed discussion of each component's role in a directory system.

Chapter 4, "Directory Planning," discusses the importance of identifying the business issues driving the implementation of a directory and describes the considerations you face in designing the structure of a directory. We also compare the use of standard objects and attributes with the design of custom objects and attributes.

Chapter 5, "Directory Technologies," provides you with a broad view of all of the applications of directories. These include host operating systems, network operating systems, electronic messaging, calendaring/scheduling, remote access, collaboration, workflow, facsimile, conferencing, and document management.

Chapter 6, "Security," starts with an overview of network security and a discussion of how directories are used to support security. We give you a more detailed discussion of the role of directories in authentication, encryption, and public key infrastructure. We describe the role of directories in other applications associated with security such as single sign-on.

Chapter 7, "Network Management," is an overview of the role of directories and directory services in network management. We also review initiatives like the Distributed Management Task Forces' Directory-Enabled Network.

Chapter 8, "Network Operating Systems," is a review of each of the major network operating systems, focusing on the structure of the embedded directory, standards support, how the directory is populated and distributed, security considerations, interfaces to other directories, availability of application program interfaces, and opportunities for integration.

Chapter 9, "Messaging and Collaboration," is a review of each of the major applications in this market, focusing on the structure of the embedded directory, standards support, how the directory is populated and distributed, underlying dependencies, security considerations, interfaces to other directories, availability of application program interfaces, and opportunities for integration.

Chapter 10, "Telephony and Video Conferencing," investigates the role of the directory in efforts to bring together voice and electronic messaging, computer-telephony integration, and video conferencing.

Chapter 11, "Meta-Directories," reviews the history of directory consolidation, the reasons why you might develop a meta-directory, and the types of meta-directories. In addition, we review the structure and function of a meta-directory, the factors you must consider in the decision to implement a meta-directory, and meta-directory design issues.

Chapter 12, "Looking Ahead," is an overview of emerging trends in directory technology and the outlook for directories in the future.

CHAPTER

1

Directories and Their Importance to the Enterprise

You may have seen articles, conferences, workshops, and vendor announcements regarding directories. Announcements for new releases of major operating systems are touting the operating systems' directory capabilities. But what are directories? How are they different from the printed directories we use in everyday life? What is it about networked computer systems that make directories so attractive and important? What are the components of a directory-enabled solution? This chapter introduces you to basic directory concepts and explains why they are important in today's enterprise computing environment.

What Is a Directory?

Directories in the networked computing world serve much the same purpose as such familiar printed directories as phone books. A directory is an information repository for data about network users, devices, and applications. Directories can be used to control the relationships between network resources and users. Directories help system users and administrators answer questions, find people and resources, identify authorized users, and maintain the integrity and security of the network.

If the directory is a repository, what kind of information does it contain? A directory can contain data about people. This data may represent the following:

- A single user
- A group of users
- A role in an organization

A directory can also contain information about resources. Here are some examples of the resources that might be included in a directory:

- Communications devices
- Network computing devices
- Printer queues
- Printers
- Fax machines
- Application programs
- Shared drives
- Search engines
- Workstations
- Services

The term *object* refers to the entry about a person or resource in the directory. A directory also contains the *attributes,* or description, of an object. For example, if an object in a directory is a person, the person's attributes may include his or her login ID, password, application access rights, contact information, and printer assignments.

Data alone does not make a directory. The information in a directory must be stored within a structure that helps make the information easy to retrieve. For example, a printed directory may store data about people as an alphabetized list, sorted by last name, within a location. This approach to organizing a directory assumes that users will access directory information based on the known location of the person and then look for a specific person with his or her surname. Directories can be structured with a wide variety of methods, each selected to support the goals of the organization using the directory. The directory and its structure are often referred to as the *namespace.*

TERMINOLOGY ALERT!

The terms *directory* and *directory services* are often used interchangeably! In this book, we use *directory* to refer to the data repository and *directory services* to refer to the methods, or protocols, used to access a directory.

What Problems Do Directories Solve?

Directories have been a part of human society in one form or another as long as people have lived together and needed to correspond. Societies developed many conventions to associate people with physical locations, such as cities, buildings, street addresses, apartment or lot numbers, and telephones, once these were invented. As populations grew, and as technology and societies evolved, methods for collecting, maintaining, and publishing this information have kept pace with these needs.

The rapid rate of change in today's world affects the way we communicate. The reach and range of our social and business relationships now extend globally and may involve hundreds or thousands of people. To satisfy our need to find things, the number of directories is growing and directory services are evolving to make the information available in ways that are meaningful. Today's challenge is that there are more and more directories, and the needs that they satisfy are becoming more and more specific, yet people and resources often have to work together globally. Resources in companies no longer subscribe to a hierarchy but may be distributed according to a matrix of needs. The changing nature of business and the ways in which information is managed and distributed in organizations are becoming increasingly complex.

Directories now exist throughout the enterprise. Directories used in computer applications are widespread and support network and host access, electronic mail, group scheduling, document management, database applications, information sharing and collaboration, and remote access. Directories may also support human resources information, contractor data, real estate resources, telephone systems and networked communications resources, security systems for building access, physical mail delivery, and many others.

In addition to making information available within an organization, directories support activities between enterprises. A business today is often viewed as a component in a supply chain, that is, as one contributor among several whose product is the result of the components each brings together. The ability to bring the right components together at the right price, or a need to share the risk in an endeavor, often results in the development of business partnerships, rather than outright mergers. In many partnerships the boundaries between organizational processes are becoming blurred, particularly as one organization's output is integrally linked as the input to another's manufacturing process.

Other cross-enterprise situations, such as mergers and acquisitions, can bring together unique companies, each with its own people and resources. Yet, the merged companies are expected to perform seamlessly soon after they start working together.

These business conditions and relationships require the ability to locate, communicate, and share information in a secure manner. Directories can improve the effectiveness of operations in each of these complex organizational models because they enable the location of resources and contain information that can facilitate business activities.

Directory Types

The technology associated with directories has evolved to satisfy many needs. In order to select the best technology for a particular problem, you must understand basic directory types. Directories fall into one of the following categories:

- Single-purpose
- Indexed
- Distributed
- Meta-directory

Single-Purpose Directories

Single-purpose directories are organized and accessed to satisfy one type of information need and are the most common directory application. Figure 1.1 shows an electronic address book. In this example of a single-purpose directory, the directory is used to locate the e-mail address associated with known names. The directory can be structured so that additional information about a person can be included, like address, title, and phone number, but the purpose of the directory is still to locate information about people. Other applications like calendars and administration programs are based on single-purpose directories.

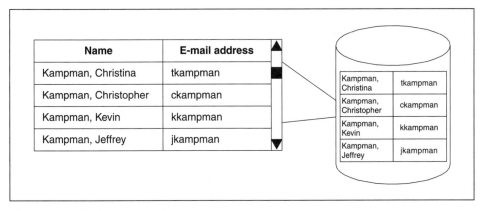

Figure 1.1 Single-purpose directory.

Indexed Directories

An index provides a specific view of directory information so that users can access information quickly. Indexes are also known as locators. For example, Figure 1.2 shows the directory a financial company may provide to support a Web application that allows customers to access the accounts they have with the company. Because financial services firms may offer many kinds of accounts that are tailored to the specific needs of the customer, the account information may be distributed across several different data stores, or repositories. The purpose of the index is to identify, for each customer, what accounts the customer has and where that information resides. The Web application references the index when the customer accesses the company's Web page, accesses the correct repository for the account requested, and presents the information from the account to the customer.

Distributed Directories

The telephone books published for all the cities in a state provide a good illustration of *distributed* directories. Each city in the state has a directory that usually contains both white pages and yellow pages. The directories may not share exactly the same format, and the directories may be published by different companies. The approach for entries in the phone books and for finding information, however, is generally the same from city to city. We consider the directories distributed because they cover a wide geographic area and serve a variety of purposes, yet they are all part of the

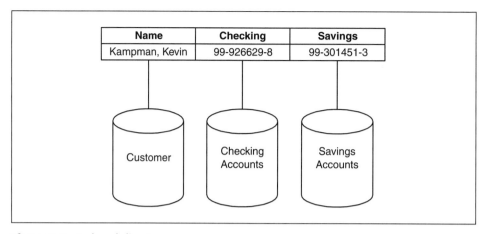

Name	Checking	Savings
Kampman, Kevin	99-926629-8	99-301451-3

Customer   Checking Accounts   Savings Accounts

Figure 1.2 Indexed directory.

same system of communications. Figure 1.3 shows a system of distributed directories.

Distributed directories in networked computing systems are similar to a collection of telephone books in a state. An entry for a single person may appear in multiple directories that support a variety of networked applications in the organization. For example, if an organization has more than one e-mail system, all of the names of people in the organization are usually included in the directories for each of the e-mail systems. Information about all of the members of an organization appears in the network operating system directory so that each person has access to the network. Finally, information about each person would appear in a calendaring system directory so that everyone can participate in group scheduling functions. Distributed directories are also known as *networks of directories.*

Organizations tie these directories together to share information between systems. In the cases of e-mail and calendaring, for example, it is important that the systems reflect all the participating individuals in the organization, whether or not that is the system that they use. This allows an individual on one system to communicate with an individual on another system, without being concerned about what system the person actually uses.

The process that ties together distributed directories is *directory synchronization,* which will be discussed further in Chapter 11, "Meta-Directories."

Meta-Directory

The concept of a web, or network, of directories, all containing the same information about similar entities, raises issues about duplication, redun-

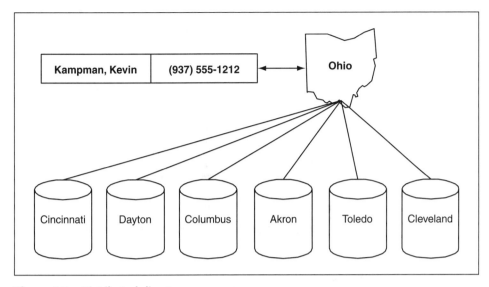

Figure 1.3   Distributed directory.

dancy, inaccuracy, and costs of administration. As a response to these issues, object management and information consolidation approaches are becoming popular. The Burton Group coined the term *meta-directory* in 1996
to identify how technology could be used to resolve some of these issues.

The concept of a meta-directory is based on collecting all of the information associated with a single object or entity in one place, as shown in Figure 1.4. A meta-directory is based on a relational algebra concept, the *join*,
where information about a single object that resides in multiple entries can
be joined, or combined, into one entry. The join is based on the condition
that the entries that represent the object have some characteristic, like
name, that can be used to uniquely and unambiguously pair the entries together. Figure 1.5 shows a typical join operation.

By accomplishing the join, making information available to a number of
different sources for a variety of purposes becomes possible. The meta-
directory becomes a multi- or general-purpose directory. It does not assume responsibility for the information that it represents, however. This is
still the responsibility of the contributing directory, or *authoritative* source.
The meta-directory acts primarily as a clearinghouse for other directories.

A meta-directory is also distinguished from single-purpose directories
because it does not always contain all the information about an entity or object. The information represented in a meta-directory may be dynamic,
available only when it is required. If two single-purpose directories contain
the same information about an object, for example, a telephone number,

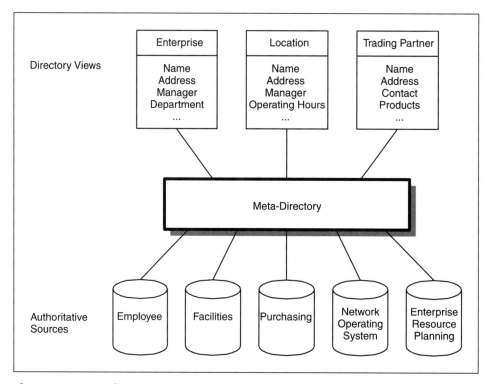

Figure 1.4   Meta-directory.

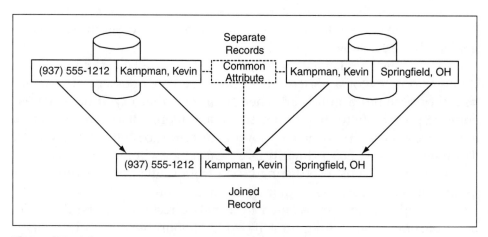

Figure 1.5   Join.

WHAT'S THE DIFFERENCE BETWEEN A DIRECTORY AND A DATABASE?

A directory seems like just another database—how is it different from ordinary database applications? It's true that a directory is a database, but it's a database with a specific function and purpose. A directory stores information that tends to be relatively static. The structure that's used to store the information meets the preconceived notions about how it will be accessed by its community of users. The structure is stable and is rarely changed. Finally, directory records are usually accessed on a read-only basis. Compare this to a typical database application that usually has a specific purpose and whose content changes with each transaction it records. The structure of a database can also change more often than a directory's because it changes to meet the needs of the application that relies on it.

this represents duplication and redundancy. If an inquiry is made to a meta-directory for the telephone number associated with an entry, the return of that information may be the result of the retrieval of that information from the authoritative source.

Multiple directories containing the same information about people and resources are expensive and prone to inaccuracy. The meta-directory approach is popular because it represents the information about entities and objects in a consistent way, simplifies the collection and distribution of the information throughout the organization, and can be employed to eventually reduce the number of single-purpose directories in an organization.

Beyond the Repository

The information in a directory is of no value to an organization unless it can be used. Figure 1.6 shows the other elements that must be in place to make the data in a directory accessible and usable. A total directory solution consists of the repository, directory services, and directory-enabled applications.

What Are Directory Services?

Directory services are access protocols and techniques that allow software tools to access directory information. The software tools may retrieve

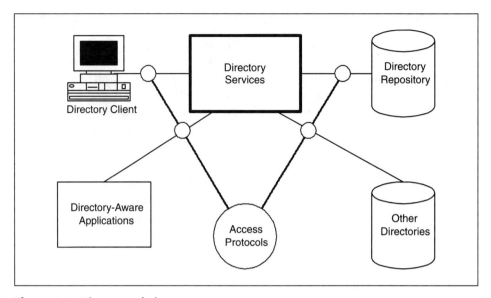

Figure 1.6 Directory solution components.

directory information and use it to accomplish a wide variety of tasks. Directory services provide a common interface to the widely diverse data that might be stored in a directory. If a standardized method for accessing directory information did not exist, organizations would not benefit from the data stored in directories.

The access mechanisms provided by a directory service usually take one of two forms: standardized functions available for use to application programs or application program interfaces so that directory functionality can be directly incorporated into applications by software developers. Most commercial directory services also provide a management layer so that directory information can be entered, secured, and distributed over multiple repositories and modified as needed.

All of the functions provided by directory services are based on a set of protocols and access techniques that usually conform to standards agreed to by the network computing community. The implementation of these standards can vary from one vendor's product to another. The protocols used in a directory service can either be based on industry standards or be proprietary to a vendor. The techniques used to access directory information can also vary, with some techniques embedded in the software and others based on a Web browser or electronic mail client.

Directory services are produced by a diverse group of vendors, each of which provides a variety of standard and custom approaches for using directory information.

Directory-Enabled Applications

Directory-enabled applications rely on directory services and the directory to provide a specific set of functions.

Automation technology is increasingly integrated over networks. Applications and services are distributed in multitier client/server environments that are infinitely more complex than the host-based systems of the past. Directory-enabled applications and directory services are a key component of this automation infrastructure, enabling access to systems and information, facilitating the location of information and resources, and providing support for administration and security. Directories in this automation infrastructure store information about virtual private networks (VPNs), virtual local area networks (VLANs), and IP addresses.

Directory-enabled applications and directory services may be used to enforce network policies and service-level agreements for one server, across a network, and between networks. For example, the information in a directory about a user can limit the user's access to one server or give the user access to resources across an entire network. Some vendors' products allow an administrator to synchronize passwords between networks. A directory-enabled application may include tools that allow administrators to publish directory information and to use directory information to print network management reports.

Directory-enabled applications help users locate print and file servers and help administrators manage system inventory and software configurations. Network administrators can use directory-enabled applications to distribute software, provide version control, and handle updates to applications or workstation operating systems.

Some additional directory-enabled applications include these:

- Digital signature verification
- Remote dial-in access authorization
- Single sign-on to a network

Directory-enabled applications are becoming crucial components of networked applications and services. They are another example of how essential directories can be to the operation of an enterprise.

TERMINOLOGY ALERT!

The functions performed by *directory services* and *directory-enabled applications* working together are often lumped together under the term *directory services.*

Directories and the Enterprise

The boundaries within and between organizations have blurred, resulting in open enterprises. Open enterprises require the ability to exchange information at the interpersonal, application, and network levels, always preserving and protecting the interests of the organizations at the same time. Directory-related technology can contribute by setting up or merging information at each of these levels in a manner appropriate to the needs of each. A directory is the basis for organizing participants and improving communications.

Directories can contribute to improving security within and between organizations by the development of a shared and consistent repository about personnel, assets, and resources. For example, in many organizations, the hiring and termination processes are distributed across multiple systems, including human resources, systems administration, asset management, and others. Providing access to all of these resources at the time someone is hired is a problem for many organizations because the processes are rarely integrated. When an employee is hired it may take several weeks for all of the tools necessary for the employee to do his or her job function to be allocated or assigned. This represents a serious productivity issue for any organization, particularly when you consider that annual employee turnover in many large organizations exceeds 15 percent.

The termination of an employee may be equally problematic. Termination of an employee includes collecting company assets, restricting access to organizational resources, termination of accounts and privileges, and archiving of sensitive information. To protect itself, an organization terminating an employee should complete these procedures in a timely manner. In reality, however, there is rarely a coordinated effort to address all of these requirements. Organizations can use a directory to identify all assets and access that should be managed as part of the termination process, including public and private keys.

As organizations rely more and more on the Internet for communications, secure communications become even more important. Components of secure communications at the network level rely on key exchange mechanisms to set up encrypted communications. At the application level, the need to authorize access, authenticate users, ensure integrity, assert nonrepudiation of transactions, and maintain confidentiality using digital certificates also requires a certificate handling mechanism. These activities are examples of the role that public key infrastructure plays in secure communications. Although there are other components to a public key infrastructure, the directory serves as the perfect storage and access mechanism for certificate management on a large scale.

Distributed client/server computing introduces new levels of complexity based on the distribution of applications, information sharing mechanisms, and the need for secure access to applications distributed across the enterprise. The directory can be employed to publish information about application services. It is a core component of the Distributed Computing Environment (DCE) Global and Cell Directory Services, and it will also serve in a more complex role in the Microsoft Windows 2000 Active Directory. In addition, it is possible for application developers to publish configuration information in the directory for access by application clients to reduce the number of distribution points and to increase the accuracy and reliability of the information.

Summary

The ability to locate information about people and resources is a basic requirement within an organization. Because of this, directories are found in almost every manual and automated process. Directories provide an organization with the ability to manage the information associated with people and resources and are a common tool for managing and publishing information. Directories allow organizations to make more information and services on the network accessible to more users. The use of directories makes administering large, complex networked installations easier and provides mobility to networked users. Directories are becoming more widespread because users are finding new types of data to store in the repository and more applications for the data already maintained in existing directories. A consistent directory strategy across and between enterprises is becoming more critical. This is due to the changing nature of business relationships and the need for more accurate information, reduced administration costs, and better security, as well as the complexity of distributed computing platforms.

CHAPTER

2

Standards

Imagine the chaos that would reign in your home if every appliance you used required a specific type of electrical outlet with its own electrical service specifications. Standardization of both the electrical service and the requirements of the appliances has thankfully spared us from this scenario. For directories, with their multiple applications and networking environments, standards and standardization are essential in order for organizations to take full advantage of the benefits of a directory-enabled environment.

Standards do not just emerge—they require sustained cooperative effort between organizations that exist to nurture the standards and the technical community at large. This chapter discusses the purpose and goals of the organizations that produce directory standards and provides a description of the standards themselves.

Standards: Where Do They Come From?

The industry directory services standards that we are concerned with in this book are those developed by the Consultative Committee on Telephony and Telecommunications, now known as the International Telecommunications

Union (www.itu.org), and the Internet Engineering Task Force (www.ietf
.org). Notable influences on directory standards are also provided by the
Network Applications Consortium (www.netapps.org) and the Distributed
Management Task Force (www.dmtf.org).

The ITU is responsible for the development of the X.500 series of recommendations; the IETF is responsible for the Lightweight Directory Access
Protocol standards, as well as a number of related standards about networking and security.

International Telecommunications Union (ITU)

The ITU is an international organization composed of representatives from
member nations. The membership consists of, but is not limited to, the
members of the United Nations. The goal of the ITU is to facilitate peaceful
relations, cooperation among peoples, and economic and social development by means of efficient telecommunications services.

The ITU's primary purpose is to do the following:

- Maintain and extend cooperation among its members for the im-
  provement and rational use of telecommunications

- Offer technical and financial assistance to developing nations to implement telecommunications capabilities

- Promote development of technical facilities to improve the efficiency
  of telecommunication services

- Increase the usefulness of telecommunication services by making
  them available to a global public audience

- Work with business and governmental entities to facilitate the incorporation of telecommunications into the global information infrastructure

The ITU accomplishes this by managing the use of radio frequencies for
telecommunications purposes, developing and promoting communications
standards, assisting with the financing and deployment of telecommunications infrastructures in developing nations, coordinating the integration of
telecommunications facilities, and helping to manage international rate
structures for the use of those facilities.

The ITU plays an important role for directories. It initiates studies, makes
regulations, adopts resolutions, formulates recommendations and opin-
ions, and collects and publishes information concerning telecommunication matters. X.500 Directory Services, a key standard for directories, is one
of ITU's chief activities.

Internet Engineering Task Force (IETF)

The IETF is an international community of interest consisting of network designers, operators, vendors, and researchers. Formed in 1986, the IETF is concerned with the smooth operation of the Internet and the evolution of the Internet architecture. It is the principal organization tasked with the development of new Internet standards and capabilities. The IETF is an open forum; any interested individual can participate. The IETF develops recommendations and standards associated with Internet technologies. It conducts its technical work in working groups that are organized by specific areas or topics. The topics for the working groups include Applications, Internet, IP: Next Generation, Network Management, Operational Requirements, Routing, Security, Transport, and User Services. The work is generally accomplished using electronic mail distribution lists; there is no formal membership for a working group. The IETF also holds meetings three times a year.

The mission of the IETF is to do the following:

- Identify and propose solutions to problems with the Internet
- Specify how protocols are developed and used to solve problems
- Make recommendations regarding the standardization of protocols and their usage
- Facilitate technology transfer from the research arm to the wider Internet community
- Provide a forum for the exchange of information within the Internet community

There are a number of related groups that work together with the IETF. The formal structure or hierarchy consists of the following groups:

- The Internet Society (ISOC) and its Board of Trustees
- The Internet Activities Board (IAB)
- The Internet Engineering Steering Group (IESG)
- The IETF itself

The Internet Society is a group of professionals concerned with the growth and evolution of the worldwide Internet, the way in which it is used, and the entire range of social, political, and technical issues associated with it. The ISOC Trustees approve appointments to the IAB based on nominations submitted by the IETF.

The Internet Activities Board is a technical advisory group of the ISOC. It provides oversight of the Internet architecture and its protocols. It also provides an appeals function to decisions made by the IESG. The IAB approves appointments to the IESG based on nominations from the IETF.

The Internet Engineering Steering Group provides technical management of IETF activities and the Internet standards process. It administers the rules and procedures ratified by the ISOC trustees. The IESG appoints area directors to manage IETF working groups. The IESG manages the entry of information into the Internet standards track, which includes the final approval of Internet Standards.

An Internet Standard is a useful, stable, well-understood, and technically competent specification that has multiple independent and interoperable implementations tested over time. These standards have significant public support.

The development of Internet Standards, as described in RFC-2026, is accomplished in the following manner. Based on an expressed need or problem, a specification is developed, tested, revised, and reviewed in an iterative process by the Internet community. When it is complete, it is adopted as a Standard and published. The factors that influence this process include the need for specifications of high technical quality, the interests of the participating parties, the need for widespread consensus, and evaluation of the utility of the specification.

The process of developing the body of knowledge that contributes to a standard is straightforward. Internet-Drafts are published as a work-in-progress, with a life cycle of six months. A draft is submitted for evaluation and comment, and it is accepted by the IESG, continues on the revision track, or is allowed to expire. If the IESG accepts a draft, it promotes it to Request for Comment (RFC) status and assigns the RFC a number. RFCs are intended to represent the specifications for a protocol or service. Some RFCs remain as RFCs; others evolve through the phases of an evaluation process and become standards.

When an RFC is selected for consideration as a standard, it is subjected to an additional evaluation process. The purpose of the evaluation process is to measure the maturity of the specification. The stages of the evaluation process are *proposed standard, draft standard,* and *standard*. Certain characteristics related to the status of testing and evaluation of a specification are associated with these labels.

Once a standard is accepted, it is assigned a standard (STD) number in addition to its original RFC number. RFCs that are not considered for standards may be assigned labels such as *experimental, historic,* or *informational*.

As you can see, not all RFCs become standards, and not all drafts become RFCs. The process is designed to allow a public review and evaluation of specifications that ultimately results in high quality and broad acceptance.

The IETF played an important role in formalizing the directory standard known as the Lightweight Directory Access Protocol (LDAP).

Network Applications Consortium (NAC)

The NAC is a group of companies and educational institutions working together to improve the interoperability of mission-critical applications in a cross-platform computing environment. The NAC collaborates to provide strategic feedback and technical requirements to the vendor community. The NAC is responsible for the development of the Lightweight Internet Person Schema, or LIPS, which is supported by most directory platforms.

Distributed Management Task Force (DMTF)

The DMTF is an organization leading the development, adoption, and unification of management standards and initiatives for desktop, enterprise, and Internet environments. The DMTF is developing the Common Information Model (CIM). CIM represents a *schema,* or information model, that identifies object classes, the attributes associated with each object class, and the relationships between objects that govern features such as the inheritance of characteristics within a hierarchy. Like all databases, a directory must be related to an information model to be useful. The information model identifies what can be stored in the directory and the characteristics of the directory's content.

Directory Standards

The ITU, IETF, and other communities of interest have developed standards for directories. The most important directory-related standards are *X.500* and *LDAP.* The following discussion is intended to help you better understand the intent and content of these standards.

X.500

X.500 is the most influential of the standards related to directory technology. Developed by the ITU in 1988, X.500 is a series of recommendations for the organization, collection, and publication of directory information. Because X.500 is intended to be an international standard, all implementations of the standard share a common set of protocols and operations, as well as an information model for the storage and representation of information. A number of development firms then implemented X.500 recommendations for directory services as products. Although X.500 does not appear in all directory-related solutions, it does represent a significant body of experience and lessons learned. The concepts embodied in X.500 have influenced many other, more recent directory solutions. Because of X.500's highly influential history, a basic understanding of X.500 is critical to understanding the inner workings of many directory solutions.

X.500 does have shortcomings. It makes rigid assumptions about geopolitical conditions and technical architectures. Implementers and users of directories have had difficulty accepting these approaches and have lobbied for alternative approaches in other standards.

In addition to the basic standard associated with the directory, X.500, the entire standard consists of 21 recommendations on specific topics surrounding the directory. For example, X.520 discusses attributes; X.521 covers objects; X.509 is concerned with security and directories. The following list contains the most relevant of the recommendations:

X.500. The Directory: Overview of concepts, models, and services.

X.501. Models.

X.509. Authentication Framework.

X.511. Abstract Service Definition.

X.518. Procedures for Distributed Operation.

X.519. Protocol Specifications.

X.520. Selected Attribute Types.

X.521. Selected Object Classes.

X.525. Replication.

X.530. Use of systems management for administration of the Directory.

X.583. Protocol Implementation Conformance Statement pro forma for the Directory access protocol.

X.584. Protocol Implementation Conformance Statement pro forma for the Directory system protocol.

X.585. Protocol Implementation Conformance Statement pro forma for the Directory operational binding management protocol.

X.586. Protocol Implementation Conformance Statement pro forma for the Directory information shadowing protocol.

The following additional recommendations are also applicable to our discussion of X.500:

X.200. Open Systems Interconnection—Basic Reference Model.

X.219. Remote Operations—Model, Notation, and Service Definition.

X.229. Remote Operations—Protocol Specification.

X.680. Open Systems Interconnection—Abstract Syntax Notation One: Specification of basic notation (ASN.1).

The text of all X.500 recommendations can be obtained for a fee from the ITU. The ITU Web site includes more information about each of the recommendations and ordering information to help you obtain the full text of the recommendations.

X.500 is an application model based on the Open Systems Interconnection (OSI) network architecture. In order to make the application more accessible, most vendors provide support for RFC-1006, which allows OSI applications to run over an Internet Protocol (IP) network. RFC-1006 provides a functional mapping at the transport layer between IP and OSI.

X.500 Architecture

A directory represents a distributed information system. This system consists of one or more directory servers under the control of a single authority or organization. This is known as the Directory Management Domain (DMD). Each of the directory servers in the Directory Management Domain is known as a Directory System Agent (DSA). Client applications or user interfaces wishing to access information in the directory do so using Directory User Agents (DUA). The information contained in the directory is known as the Directory Information Base (DIB), and the information is structured in a hierarchical format known as the Directory Information Tree (DIT).

Directory Information Tree

The DIT contains several kinds of objects and entries. Figure 2.1 shows the basic elements in the DIT. The first object is the abstract notion of the *root* of the tree, also known as Top. The next object is a container object, which contains subordinate entries or leaf objects. There are also alias entries, which are used as pointers to other leaf objects in the tree.

X.500 proposes a naming model for the hierarchy maintained in the DIT. The naming model is proposed as an annex to X.500. The naming model

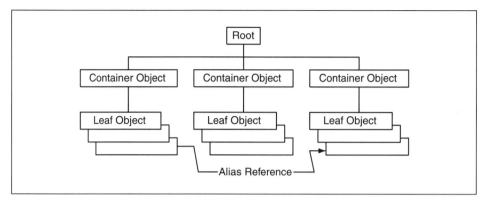

Figure 2.1 Directory Information Tree.

proposes the root, or Top of the tree, followed by Country, Locality, or Organization objects. Additional objects include Residential Person, Group of Names, Organizational Units, Organizational Persons, Organizational Roles, Application Processes, Application Entities, Devices, and so forth. Some of the objects, like Locality and Organizational Unit, can repeat, or be nested. In the case of Locality, the object can be positioned as needed beneath Country, Organization, or Organizational Unit. Country, Organization, Organizational Unit, and Locality would typically be container objects, while Residential and Organizational Person Objects would be leaf entries in the DIT. Figure 2.2 shows an example of a DIT using some of the proposed object names in the naming model.

X.500 Protocols

The directory system must describe certain protocols for the exchange of information or applications can't use the information stored in the directory. The client/server protocol used by the Directory User Agent to access information in the directory is called Directory Access Protocol (DAP). There are also several server-to-server protocols specified. The first is the Directory System Protocol (DSP). This protocol is the one most commonly used for accessing information between DSAs.

The directory is designed to provide for information distribution in order to improve performance and reliability. The capability to distribute multiple copies of information through the directory system is known as *replication*. Two protocols are associated with information replication: the Directory Information Shadowing Protocol (DISP) and the Directory Operational Binding Management Protocol (DOP). DISP allows one directory to

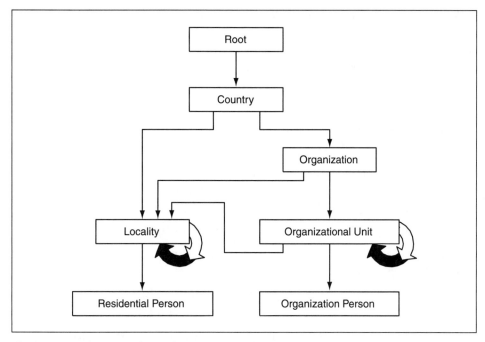

Figure 2.2   Directory Information Tree example.

obtain and maintain a copy, or shadow, of some of the elements stored in another DSA. DOP allows participating DSAs to negotiate the nature of and parameters associated with the shadowing relationship, such as the frequency of updates.

From a client perspective, X.500 DAP provides the following operations:

Directory Bind. This operation allows a DUA to establish a session with a DSA, including any necessary parameters to set up the relationship.

Directory Unbind. This operation closes the session between a DUA and a DSA.

Read. The Read operation returns all or some of the attributes associated with a specific entry in the directory.

Compare. The Compare operation allows the directory to test a provided value against the value of an attribute in an entry. It identifies whether the values match. It is commonly used to test passwords.

List. The List operation returns the names of the immediate subordinates to an entry in the directory.

Search. The Search operation returns the entries from a specified area of the DIT that match a specified criterion.

AddEntry. This operation adds a new entry to the DIT.

RemoveEntry. This operation removes an existing entry from the DIT.

ModifyEntry. This operation changes an entry's attributes or values.

Modify RDN. This operation changes the Relative Distinguished Name of a leaf entry in the DIT.

Abandon. This operation is invoked by a DUA to terminate a previously requested operation, such as a search.

The interoperation of DSAs presumes an understanding of the distribution of knowledge or information in the directory environment. Figure 2.3 shows the distribution of knowledge during DSA interoperation. Each DSA knows the following reference characteristics for the directory:

Internal. This directory represents the information held locally by the DSA.

Superior. This directory represents information that is held by or is accessible to a DSA above the current DSA in the DIT.

Subordinate. This directory represents information that is held by a DSA beneath the current DSA in the DIT.

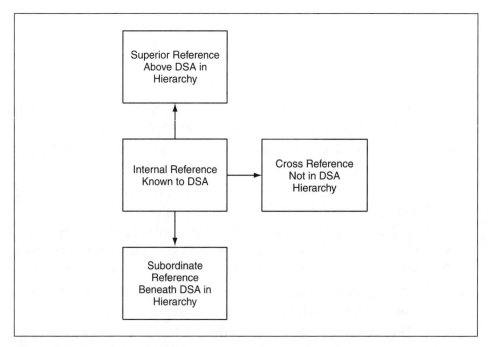

Figure 2.3   Knowledge distribution.

Cross Reference. This directory represents information that is neither superior nor subordinate to the current DSA, but is known to the current DSA.

As we mentioned earlier in this chapter, the DIT has a hierarchical organization, also known as an inverted tree. Each node, or vertex, in the tree represents a branch that leads either to other nodes or to a leaf entry in the naming context. Name resolution in the DIT is based on two procedures, finding the initial naming context and locating the entry within that context.

So that applications can conduct a search of the information stored in the directory, the DSA provides several mechanisms for locating information in the DIT. The mechanisms are known as *chaining, multicasting,* and *referral.* We'll discuss each in more detail.

Chaining. Chaining is an operation in which a query is made of one DSA when the knowledge reference is not internal. The DSA queries another DSA that knows the information. Once the initial DSA has obtained the needed information it returns the results to the DUA. Figure 2.4 shows the possible information pathways and participants in chaining.

Multicasting. Multicasting is used when a DSA does not have the information internally, so it broadcasts the query to multiple DSAs. Multicasting can be done in series or in parallel. Figure 2.5 shows how multicasting might be accomplished.

Referral. A referral is the result of a query to a DSA that does not have the information but that knows of a route to that information. It passes the route back to the inquiring DUA, which must then query the alternative source. A referral occurs when there is no bilateral agreement between DSAs for the sharing of information. Figure 2.6 shows how multiple queries and responses might be made during a referral.

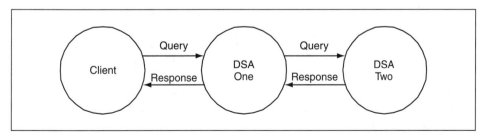

Figure 2.4 Chaining.

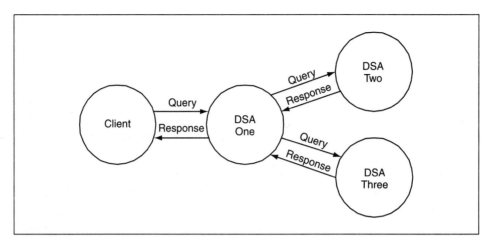

Figure 2.5   Multicasting.

The Directory System Protocol is based on service *ports,* or access points. These ports include the following:

ChainedReadPort. This port provides the ChainedRead, ChainedCompare, and ChainedAbandon operations.

ChainedSearchPort. This port provides the ChainedList and ChainedSearch operations.

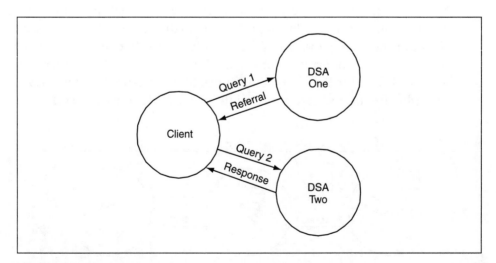

Figure 2.6   Referral.

ChainedModifyPort. This port provides the ChainedAddEntry, ChainedRemoveEntry, ChainedModifyEntry, and ChainedModify-RDN operations.

It is useful to note the correspondence between the operations chained between DSAs and the similar operations associated with the DUA and DSA.

The Lightweight Directory Access Protocol (LDAP)

In the early days of X.500, the only way to access the information in the directory was to use the native OSI network protocol stack. A protocol stack represents the levels of abstraction from the physical signals "on the wire" that allow computers to communicate to the applications that actually interpret and use this information.

The OSI protocol stack is relatively fat in comparison to IP. Because early personal computers did not have the resources to process such a large protocol stack, it was extremely difficult to implement the X.500 DUA. To solve these difficulties, the IETF proposed the RFC-1006 solution, which allows OSI applications to run over IP. Figure 2.7 shows the components of the RFC-1006 solution.

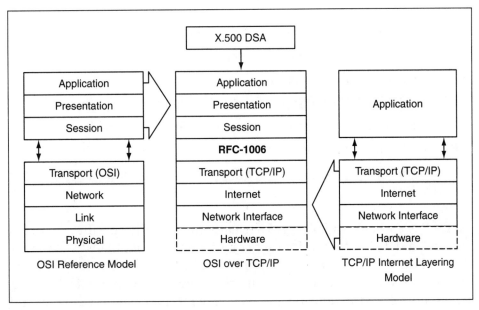

Figure 2.7 RFC-1006.

Just as with the OSI protocol stack, a full implementation of DAP in a directory client was also nearly impossible to implement within the constraints of the personal computer environment. Researchers at the University of Michigan, and later the IETF, spearheaded efforts to slim down the DAP client-to-server protocol. This effort resulted in the development of LDAP, which was designed to use the TCP/IP protocol. LDAP version 2 (RFC-1777) was published in 1996, and work began almost immediately on LDAP version 3. LDAP does not require an X.500 directory on the server; any LDAP-compliant information repository is sufficient. Because of its simplified and efficient method for accessing information, LDAP has been adopted universally by the development community. LDAP has emerged as the dominant method of client/server directory access.

LDAP, like X.500, does not specify implementation details. By this we mean that the actual implementation is solution independent. The specification identifies how the information is represented and the mechanisms for storage, access, and management. This provides high levels of interoperability, and some grounds for fine-tuning, like any standards-based solution. The crucial difference between LDAP and X.500 is that LDAP uses the same information model as X.500 but provides a simpler set of access mechanisms.

The LDAP standard consists of the following specifications, which are also available from the IETF Web site.

RFC-1777. Lightweight Directory Access Protocol.

RFC-2251. Lightweight Directory Access Protocol (v 3).

RFC-2252. Attribute Syntax Definitions.

RFC-2253. UTF-8 String Representation of Distinguished Names.

RFC-2254. The String Representation of LDAP Search Filters.

RFC-2255. The LDAP URL Format.

RFC-2256. A Summary of the X.500(96) User Schema for use with LDAPv3.

LDAP is constantly evolving. The standard currently specifies an access protocol, a data file format for exchanging information, LDAP Data Interchange Format (LDIF), and an Application Program Interface (API). The directory community is doing additional work related to replication and access control, and standards should emerge for these over the next several years.

LDAP Data Interchange Format (LDIF)

The LDAP standard describes a data interchange format known as LDIF. The LDIF format is very straightforward. The basic format for an entry is this:

[id]

dn: entryDN

attrtype: attrvalue

...

{blank line separator between entries}

An *id* is an optional numeric entry, the *entryDN* is the LDAP distinguished name (DN of the directory entry), the *attrtype* is an LDAP attribute type, and the *attrvalue* is the value for the *attrtype*. For example, if we wanted to import information into an existing directory, the LDIF format for an entry might appear as follows:

dn: Kevin Kampman

address: 757 Peshek Lane

city: Springfield

state: Ohio

postalCode: 45506-4209

e-mail: kkampman@tbg.com

LDAP version 2 was designed to access X.500 (1988) directories. The protocol is based on the exchange of parameterized LDAP Messages and LDAP Responses. Version 2 did not incorporate the capability for referrals to another directory data source, and it supported only simple and Kerberos authentication of clients. LDAP version 3 provides support for all version 2 protocol elements and incorporates additional authentication mechanisms, such as Simple Authentication and Security Layer (SASL), as well as support for referrals. Version 3 has extended features such as adding new operations and adding additional controls to existing operations. The LDAP schema is published in the directory to enable schema discovery, or the interpretation of customized schemas. This feature helps to improve interoperability both between servers and between clients and servers.

LDAP Client Operations

LDAP provides the following client operations, which are comparable to the same X.500 DAP operations. The functionality of the X.500 Read and List operations are satisfied by the LDAP Search operation:

Bind. The Bind operation authenticates the client to the directory and establishes a session.

Search. The Search operation returns a list of entries that meet the provided search criteria.

Compare. The Compare operation identifies that a corresponding stored value for an attribute is equal to a supplied value, without revealing the content of the stored value, for example, a password.

Add. The Add operation inserts a new entry into the directory.

Delete. The Delete operation removes an existing entry from the directory.

Modify. The Modify operation changes an entry's attributes or values.

ModifyRDN. The ModifyRDN operation changes the value of the Relative Distinguished Name of a leaf entry, similar to modifying the key field(s) in a database entry.

Abandon. The Abandon operation terminates a previously submitted request, such as a Search inquiry.

In summary, LDAP has received widespread support and is being adopted by all major directory and directory-dependent applications. IBM and Oracle, in the database community, have also supported LDAP. LDAP is equally well suited to supporting both direct client access and applications. Future enhancements to LDAP include paged search results, sorted search results, and persistent searches. LDAP lacks the access controls and replication capabilities of X.500, but ongoing work in the standards community is focusing attention on these issues.

Other Standards Related to Directories

While X.500 and LDAP are the dominant standards related to directories, other standards do play a part in a complete directory solution. This section presents two standards related to directories, ASN.1 and TCP/IP, and a brief discussion of other emerging standards.

Abstract Syntax Notation 1 (ASN.1)

ASN.1 is a recognized standard for describing messages exchanged between computer systems. It is specified in ITU recommendation X.680. In the directory environment, ASN.1 provides the logical representation of the information exchanged between directories and directory clients. ASN.1 is used to develop an Object Identifier, a hierarchical numeric representation of the object. The hierarchy defines the registration authority, the standard employed, the object class or attribute type, and the specific object or attribute name. For example, the X.500 Person ASN.1 object class notation is 2.5.6.6, where the following applies:

2 stands for "Joint-ISO-CCITT"

2.5 stands for "ds" (directory standards)

2.5.6 stands for "Object Class"

2.5.6.6 stands for "Object Class Person"

Similarly, the ASN.1 Common Name attribute identifier is 2.5.4.3, where the following applies:

2 stands for "Joint-ISO-CCITT"

2.5 stands for "ds" (directory standards)

2.5.4 stands for "AttributeType"

2.5.4.3 stands for "AttributeType CommonName"

Standard objects and attributes are registered. This registration helps to ensure that the development community understands the standard objects and attributes. If an organization decides that it wants to define its own object classes and attributes, these can be registered or remain unregistered. Registering the objects helps to ensure interoperability between organizations and applications. Objects and attributes can be registered in the United States with the American National Standards Institute (ANSI), which issues an Object Identifier for a fee.

In the event that an organization decides not to register its objects and attributes, the properties of object inheritance help to provide interoperability. For example, if an organization defines an object class called "End-to-End Organization Person" and determines that it is a subclass of the class Organization Person, then the characteristics and attributes associated with Organization Person can be shared with other communities, even if the customizations aren't recognized. This supports the case for building custom objects using predefined object classes and attributes as templates.

Transmission Control Protocol/Internet Protocol (TCP/IP)

While TCP/IP is not a directory protocol, it is the network protocol that supports many of the directory services and other applications described in this book. The development of TCP/IP was initially funded by the Defense Advanced Research Projects Agency (DARPA). TCP/IP is a set of network standards that specifies the details of how computers communicate, as well as conventions for connecting networks and routing traffic within and between them. Today, TCP/IP is the basis for the Internet and one of the most popular networking protocols. For additional information on TCP/IP, refer to *Illustrated TCP/IP* by Matthew Naugle (Wiley, 1999).

Other Emerging Standards

Another area of interest in the directory community is multiprotocol access support. Due to the database community's interest in directories, servers that support DAP and LDAP, standard protocols like Open Database Connectivity (ODBC) or Structured Query Language (SQL), as well as proprietary vendor-specific protocols, will become common.

Extensible Markup Language (XML) may also emerge as a key technology in the directory marketplace with the identification of Directory XML (DirXML). XML provides a mechanism to describe as well as to publish information; DirXML may serve as a mechanism for publishing, exchanging, and providing interoperability between directory services and other information repositories.

Summary

Today, X.500 and LDAP represent the core directory services protocols in use in the computer and communications industries. Many large-scale enterprise directories today use X.500 products. A growing number are using LDAP-based directories as well. A number of other directory solutions are proprietary, but all X.500 and most proprietary directories support the use of LDAP as an access protocol. Later chapters of this book provide a discussion of both Microsoft Active Directory and Novell Directory Services, both of which use proprietary engines but provide LDAP access. Because the X.500 information model is a key component of the LDAP service model, it appears that the solutions of the future will continue to present the best characteristics of each standard.

Directory Basics

Building a directory is much like building a house: good planning and an effective design of the underlying structure lead to success with the finished product. The goal of this chapter is to strengthen your understanding of a directory's foundation before you undertake the process of designing a directory and organizing the information you plan to store in it.

This chapter discusses what information to store in a directory and how the information should be structured and named. You will read introductory presentations about an information architecture, developing an information model or schema, and naming the entities stored in the directory so that they are unique and can be added and retrieved in a meaningful way. Chapter 3 also introduces access and management approaches and application program interfaces so that you have a basic understanding of these aspects of a directory solution.

Directory System Operation

Before we begin our discussion of the components that make up a directory system, let's review how a directory system processes a request for directory information.

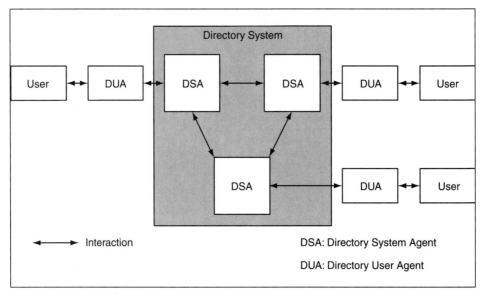

Figure 3.1   Request for directory information.

Figure 3.1 shows the components of a request for directory information. Assume that a user needs to obtain someone's telephone number from a corporate directory. The user places the request using a client-based application, known as a Directory User Agent (DUA). The company may have one or more servers devoted to directories, each of them known as a Directory System Agent (DSA). The client-based application queries a DSA containing directory information in order to retrieve the desired telephone number. The DSA replies to the DUA with the telephone number. The DUA then displays the telephone number to the user.

Even this simple transaction relies on an array of standards, protocols, information, security checkpoints, and application programs that we'll refer to as directory components. The next section discusses each directory component in more detail.

Directory Components

What works together to deliver a telephone number from a corporate directory to a user? A directory is made up of a number of different components. The key components of a directory solution like our example include technical specifications and protocols, an information architecture, application program interfaces, and management tools.

Technical Specifications and Protocols

Technical specifications and protocols are the guidelines that must be followed for interoperability and consistency across networks. Technical specifications and protocols consist of generally accepted approaches for the following:

- Client and server access protocols
- Data replication and distribution
- Security

Client and server access protocols provide a common framework for the interactions between the DUA and the DSA. If more than one server contains directory information, multiple DSAs may also need to interact with each other. Figure 3.2 shows how the DUA and DSAs communicate. Depending on the implementation, these interactions are based on the X.500 or LDAP standards (discussed in Chapter 2, "Standards,") as well as data replication and distribution. Security is also covered by standards; we'll discuss security standards in Chapter 6, "Security."

Information Architecture

An information architecture is the foundation of the directory solution— the worth of the information in a directory and the ability to access it is,

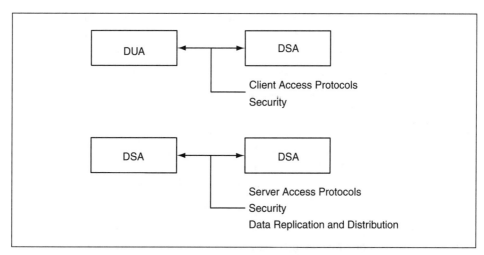

Figure 3.2 Technical specifications and protocols.

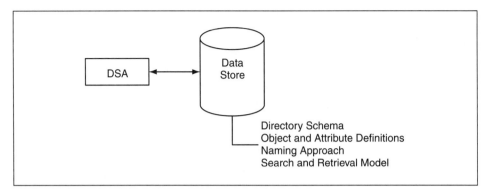

Figure 3.3   Information architecture.

after all, the point of the whole system. The actual contents and structure of the directory are defined by the information architecture. The elements of an information architecture include the following:

- Information store
- Directory schema
- Object and attribute definitions
- Naming approach
- Search and retrieval model

Figure 3.3 shows a DSA accessing an information store and its elements.

Application Program Interfaces

Application program interfaces are standard, predictable routines available to application developers so that they can write application programs that access and use the information stored in the directory. Application program interfaces are defined in the standards for directory services. Figure 3.4 shows a DSA using an API.

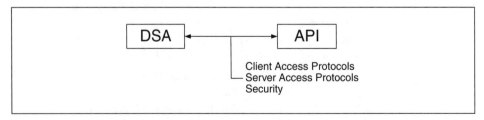

Figure 3.4   Application Program Interfaces.

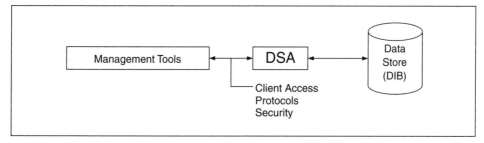

Figure 3.5   Management tools.

Management Tools

The software used to maintain the information stored in the directory is known as management tools. Most management tools are provided by directory services vendors in their directory administration software. Figure 3.5 shows management tools in action.

Now that we've defined the components of a directory, let's take a look at each one in more detail.

Information Architecture

A complete information architecture for directory services includes a place to store information, a mechanism to describe the information that is stored there, a method to ensure that each entry stored is unique, and a strategy that enables flexible information retrieval.

Information Store

The central component of a directory is the *information store,* also known as the repository or the Directory Information Base (DIB). An information store can be used to store data about people or network resources. The data in the information store is essential to all directory-enabled applications.

What to Store

Like any computer-based tool used to collect large amounts of data, a directory does not make any assumptions about the kinds of information that are included in it. You can think of the information store as a sheet of ruled paper—you supply the content as you write on the paper.

The information stored in a directory should be informative and stable and should suit a specific purpose. For example, if you were interested in using a directory as an index about customer information, you might determine that you need to keep contact information and information about the accounts the customer has with you in the directory. This could be used as a quick lookup mechanism for a Web application that presents a customized welcome screen to the customer.

It might appear to be helpful to store the customer's most recent account balance in a directory entry, but this can cause problems with the stability of the directory. A good rule of thumb when considering what information is to be stored in the directory is that if the information is dynamic and readily accessible by referencing it in the directory, then leave the information in its original location and supply a reference to it. Referencing data rather than including it in the information store helps simplify the construction and maintenance of the directory and minimizes redundancy. It is much more desirable to populate the directory with keys to the information, rather than the information itself.

As you try to decide what information to store, it is important to consider how the information will be used. There are many concerns to take into account, particularly privacy and security when you are considering information about people and organizations.

Directory Schema

In the dictionary, *schema* is defined as a pattern or a schematic diagram. As an example, consider the legend on a road map. It identifies the different kinds of roads, intersections, and geographical features that the map describes. Using the legend, we can identify the type and nature of roads leading from our origin to our destination.

The *directory schema* describes the framework or structure of the directory's information store. A directory schema may also be referred to as a Directory Information Tree (DIT). A schema functions much like the legend on a map. When applied to directories, a schema describes the Directory Information Tree, the objects in the tree, and the attributes of the objects. By following the Search and Retrieval model associated with the schema, we can traverse the DIT and locate the appropriate entries of interest to us.

If you are trying to decide what should be present in a schema, you can use the generalized models contained in the standards related to directories. These models describe information about people and resources. Most organizations, however, find the general models incomplete or unable to meet an organization's specific needs. For this reason, the directory schema suggested in the standards are extensible and can be modified to accommodate a number of requirements. Most organizations start with the generalized models and build on them to meet specific needs. Just as with the contents of the information store, the structure chosen for a directory should be stable and unchanging. Getting the structure of the DIT right is an important factor in successful directory design.

Schemas are described in several forms. Often, a top-level view is employed to show how the information stored by the directory is to be categorized. Figure 3.6 shows a top-level view of a schema using the names suggested in the standard.

A more detailed view of the schema then describes each of these categories, including the object definitions and attributes associated with each object. Figure 3.7 shows a detailed view of the schema first shown in Figure 3.6.

Hierarchies and Directories

Hierarchies are a traditional mechanism for representing many collections of information, such as families, governments, and organizations. A hierarchical perspective has also been applied to directories. The hierarchy employed with directories is also known as an *inverted tree* because a graphic representation of a directory's hierarchy looks like an upside-down tree. Using an inverted tree seems overly simplified, but we will discover that there are many factors that complicate this model.

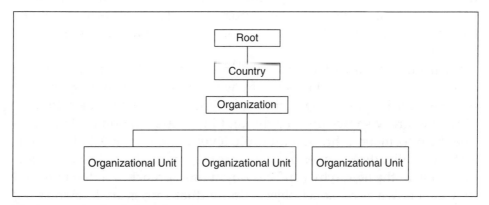

Figure 3.6 Top-level view of a schema.

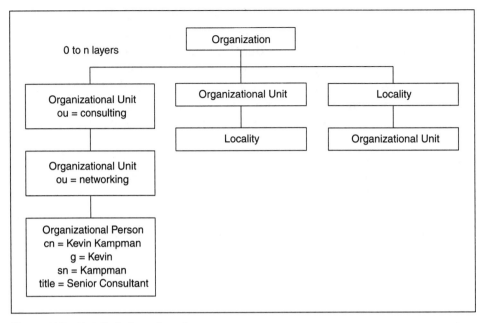

Figure 3.7   Detailed view of a schema.

When you construct the directory schema, you need to establish what kind of hierarchy will be used to model the information. Hierarchies can be *flat* or *deep*. These terms refers to the number of levels or branches that exist in the inverted tree. An inverted tree with few levels is considered flat; an inverted tree with many levels is considered deep. Organizations choose flat or deep hierarchies depending on the business and technical needs they are trying to meet. The goal of directory schema design is to keep the schema as flat as possible, but still allow physical distribution of the information and support for its usability across multiple platforms.

What does the inverted tree used in directories look like? Consider Figure 3.8. At the top of the hierarchy we establish a *root*, or beginning of the tree. This is the starting point for finding information. The next level of the hierarchy shows the tree divided into classification units that refine the information through multiple levels. The final level of the hierarchy contains directory entries, or records, themselves. The classification units in the hierarchy can be thought of as branches in the tree, and they are known as *container* objects. Individual entries are known as *leaf* objects.

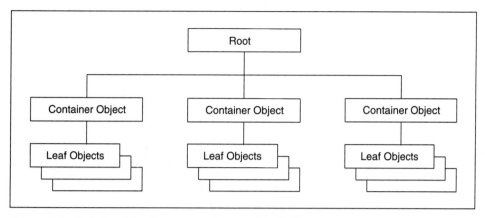

Figure 3.8 Relationship of root, container, and leaf objects.

Example: Directory Information Tree

Hierarchies can be structured based on a variety of perspectives. In the world of directories and organizations, the most common perspectives used for building the Directory Information Tree are organizational and geographical.

As an example, let's model a manufacturing firm called End-to-End. You may find it helpful to follow our discussion using Figure 3.9. The principal departments that make up the organization are R&D, Sales, Production, Human Resources, and Accounting. End-to-End's headquarters are in Cleveland; Cleveland is also home to a manufacturing plant. End-to-End has other departments in three main locations: Cleveland, Philadelphia, and Tulsa. End-to-End also has sales offices located in close proximity to customers in Newark, Cleveland, Detroit, Chicago, and Phoenix.

The starting point of our sample hierarchy contains the name of the organization. After that simple act, the decisions must begin. Do we structure the DIT first by location or by department?

If we build a schema based on department, the next level in the hierarchy elaborates the departments in the organization: R&D, Sales, Production, Human Resources, and Accounting. In the schema, each of the departments becomes a container object.

After we determine the department container objects, let's use a geographic approach to the next level in the hierarchy. Each of End-to-End's geographic locations becomes a container object. R&D, Human Resources, and Accounting are all located in Cleveland, with no other locations. Cleveland is the only container object needed for these departments; there is no

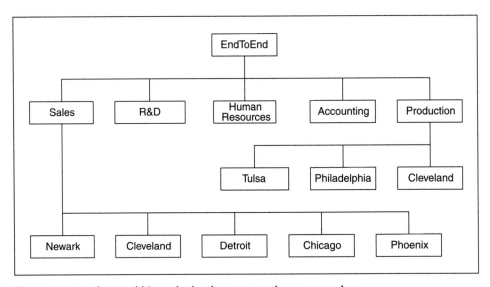

Figure 3.9   End-to-End hierarchy by department then geography.

need to divide this level of the hierarchy any further. Production needs a container object for each of its plant locations, so Cleveland, Philadelphia, and Tulsa are established as container objects at the next level of the hierarchy below Production. The Sales portion of the hierarchy needs a container object for each of the cities having a sales office: Newark, Cleveland, Detroit, Chicago, and Phoenix. Using the organizational approach to the hierarchy first, followed by divisions in the hierarchy based on geography, produces a relatively simple representation of an organization.

See Figure 3.10 for an alternative structure of the DIT for End-to-End. Schema design might incorporate location as the first level of container objects, followed by containers on the second level based on department. Using this approach results in a first level with the cities Cleveland, Philadelphia, Tulsa, Newark, Detroit, Chicago, and Phoenix as container objects. The container objects beneath Cleveland are R&D, Sales, Production, Human Resources, and Accounting. The container object beneath Philadelphia and Tulsa is Production. The container object beneath Newark, Detroit, Chicago, and Phoenix is Sales.

The preceding discussion illustrates just two of the possible approaches to structuring a hierarchy for End-to-End. See Figure 3.11 for yet another approach. We could build a flat hierarchy that included a People container and containers for each of the business functions. If we were interested only

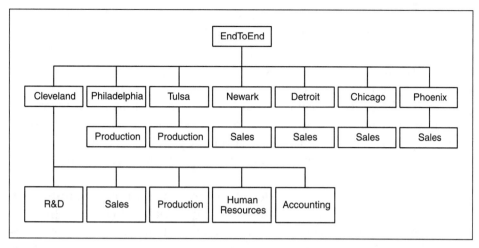

Figure 3.10   End-to-End hierarcy by geography then department.

in publishing information about people, we could establish only a People container. Because so many workable possibilities for the schema exist, the selection of a best approach for a directory is based solely on the needs and objectives of the organization designing the schema. Chapter 4, "Directory Planning," explores the issues affecting schema design in more detail.

Other Schema Design Issues

The X.500 Object Model on which the previous schema design discussion is based, assumes a global, distributed directory perspective, with divisions by country. In part, this approach emerged because the International Telecommunications Union (ITU) developed the X.500 standard. The ITU is highly influenced by the needs of the telecommunications

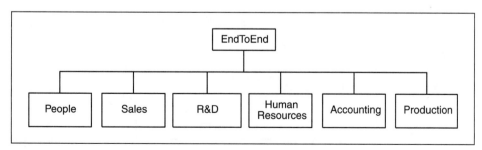

Figure 3.11   End-to-End hierarchy by people and departments.

industry, and the telecommunications industry is divided by country. What all participants discovered very quickly was that a country-based perspective did not readily map to the needs of global organizations, particularly multinational corporations. Putting Organization beneath the root of the tree instead of Country was one attempt to resolve this problem. This solution, however, soon raised another issue: Now organizations would have to register the company name in all of the participating countries. Because this solution isn't practical, organizations are seeking other approaches to schema design to address multinational concerns.

As a result, a new schema design approach is quickly gaining approval: adoption of the hierarchical naming associated with the Internet Domain Name System (DNS) at the top level of the tree. Using this approach has the advantage of hierarchical naming using an internationally recognized registration authority. Here's how it works. Let's say the domain name for our sample company is endtoend.com. The two components of the domain name are endtoend and com, for the commercial top-level naming managed by the InterNIC. See Figure 3.12 for the mapping of these DNS components into the hierarchy at the top level of the tree.

Because using the Internet Domain Name System components as part of a schema design is an effective approach, it is becoming much more widespread than the use of the X.500 Object Model.

The structure of the DIT is strongly influenced by the standards issued by organizations in the directory community. For more information about standards and standards bodies, refer to Chapter 2, "Standards."

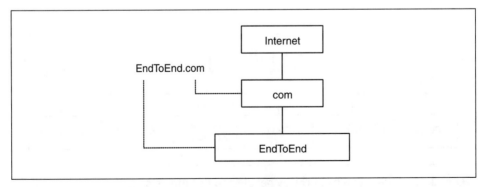

Figure 3.12 Using a domain name in a schema.

Object Attributes and Definitions

A directory stores information about entities such as people and resources. This information is modeled using the concept of *objects.* Objects in a directory are equivalent to records in a database. Like fields in a database record, the attributes maintained in an object contain detailed information about each person or resource. Attributes consist of a *type,* or name, and an *assertion,* or value. Objects also contain information about their characteristics such as access controls for management and security. The directory is object-oriented, so features like the inheritance of characteristics from parent object classes are available to directory structure designers.

If every organization that wanted to publish information in a directory had to develop its own definitions for objects and attributes, the process would be costly and cumbersome. The ITU and IETF have established standard objects and attributes for the representation of people and resources. The standard objects and attributes are generally applicable and comprehensive, but they don't cover every contingency. For this reason, mechanisms are included to extend the information model to meet the needs of individual organizations.

Some of the standard schema contributions are the Network Applications Consortium Lightweight Internet Person Schema, and the Internet White Pages Schema (RFC-2218). Other standard schema are described in the ITU standards X.520 and X.521, The Cosine and Internet X.500 Schema (RFC-1274), LDAP (RFC-2256), and draft-ietf-asid-inetorgperson-01.txt. The Distributed Management Task Force is developing the Common Information Model to describe a number of resources for the purpose of system management using directories.

As an example, some of the standard object classes in X.521 include the following:

Country	Residential Person
Locality	Application Process
Organization	Application Entity
Organizational Unit	Device
Person	MHS* User Agent
Organizational Person	MHS* User
Organizational Role	MHS* MTA
Group of Names	MHS* MS

Message Handling System

As an example, some of the standard attributes described in X.520 include the following:

Object Class	Serial Number
Common Name	State or Province Name
Country Name	Organization Unit Name
Locality Name	Title
Street Address	Telephone Number
Organization Name	Facsimile Number
Business Category	Presentation Address
Postal Address	See Also*

An alias reference to another directory entry

Chapter 4, "Directory Planning," contains more detailed information about using standard objects and attributes and designing your own objects and attributes.

Naming Approach

We've spent a fair amount of time discussing the role of the hierarchy in schema design. The ultimate design of the directory schema is reflected in the representation of people and resources. How well a schema is designed has many implications, both for searching the directory and finding entries and on the names of the entries themselves. One of the goals of a directory schema is to keep the names of the entries as compact as possible while ensuring uniqueness, making the information accessible, and meeting the objectives of the organization.

Distinguished Name

Each record, or leaf entry, in a directory has a unique name, known as the *distinguished name* (DN). The distinguished name is the collection of all the elements in the hierarchy used to construct the entry name. In the example shown in Figure 3.9, the hierarchy had the following levels:

- Company
- Department
- Location

The corresponding X.521 object class names for these levels of the hierarchy are these:

- Organization
- Organizational Unit
- Locality

Remember that the Accounting department at End-to-End is located in Cleveland, so the distinguished name for the Accounting department is as follows:

Organization = End-to-End

Organizational Unit = Accounting

Locality = Cleveland

If we wanted to add information about employees to the directory, we must add another element, a leaf object, to the schema. The leaf object contains the name of employees; its X.521 Object Class name would be Organizational Person. Leaf objects must have an attribute name to make them unique so the X.520 standard attribute name used for this example is Common Name.

So, if End-to-End's directory contained information about an accountant named John Smith, Figure 3.13 shows the distinguished name for his entry in the directory, starting just below the root of the inverted tree.

Each of the X.521 object class and X.520 attribute names can be abbreviated. Figure 3.14 shows the abbreviated form of the distinguished name for John Smith's entry in the directory.

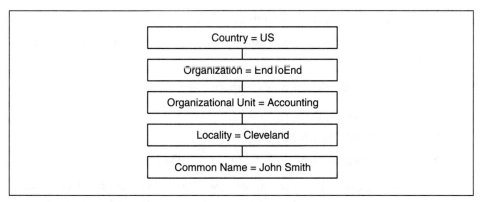

Figure 3.13 Distinguished name for John Smith.

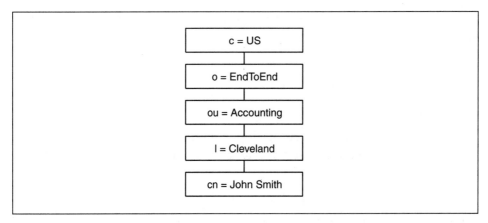

Figure 3.14 Abbreviated distinguished name for John Smith.

Relative Distinguished Name

The component of the distinguished name that ensures the uniqueness of the entry is known as the *relative distinguished name* (RDN). Actually, each individual element of the distinguished name is an RDN for that level in the hierarchy, but in practice the single element or combination of elements that ensures uniqueness is referred to as the RDN.

In the John Smith example, the RDN is the Common Name (cn) portion of the distinguished name. In practice, and particularly when the hierarchy is flat, Common Name is usually not sufficient to ensure uniqueness except in smaller organizations. To ensure uniqueness, the team developing the schema around a naming approach can do the following:

- Add depth to the hierarchy
- Use a unique identifier for each entry in the directory
- Combine the common name with a unique identifier to construct the RDN

Here are some examples of RDN approaches:

RDN = UniqueID = 123456

RDN = cn = "John Smith 123456"

RDN = cn = "John Smith" + UniqueID = 123456

Using an attribute other than Common Name as the Relative Distinguished Name raises a number of issues. First of all, adding information like a unique identification to the common name is usually not meaningful, and it can be distracting to directory users. The concatenation or construction of a complex RDN that includes nonmeaningful information raises this issue as well. In addition, the inclusion of information that is not readily associated with the entry may raise legal issues in some industries. If the information is used by client applications, adding data to the common name may cause interoperability issues. Finally, in order to implement a unique identifier you may have to develop a custom attribute, which you may have to register and otherwise maintain.

As you can see, developing a unique naming approach for directory entries requires significant analysis of the issues and implications surrounding each approach. Since each approach involves tradeoffs, we recommend taking the time to investigate the advantages and disadvantages of each approach. The simplest approach is usually the most acceptable, but what is simple in appearance often belies the large effort expended to arrive at the approach. Keep in mind that once the RDN is implemented, changing it will be a difficult task. Such a basic change to the structure of the directory can have a significant impact on directory-enabled applications such as Public Key Infrastructure that rely on the RDN.

Search and Retrieval Model

Finding information in the directory is often a daunting task. Generally, the simpler the design, the easier it is to find information. In order to retrieve information, the client application must establish a search base that identifies the root or starting point from which to begin the search.

Let's consider an example. Suppose that End-to-End has decided to place the information about all of its employees into a container called People, as shown in Figure 3.15. The search base for a directory client for End-to-End employees in this case is as follows:

Organization = End-to-End

Organizational Unit = People

Many organizations have successfully implemented a simple approach like this one. As organizations become larger and more complex, however, many new issues arise when a simple approach is present. A large organization probably employs more than one person named John Smith. In order to retrieve information about the correct John Smith, some additional identifying data has to be added to the directory entry such as a number to the name or a UniqueID to the RDN. Another approach that can be used,

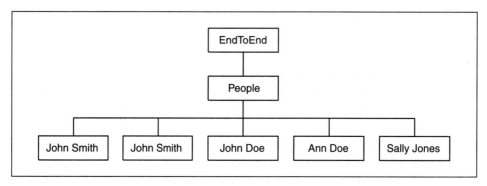

Figure 3.15 Flat hierarchy.

but that has limited viability, is to add another level to the RDN, such as Locality or Department.

Even though the naming approach may appear to solve the uniqueness problem, another issue, partitioning, remains. A *partition* refers to a division of information; the division may be logical, physical, or both. The example we used in the directory schema discussion contains several logical partitions. For example, when the schema distinguished between sales offices in different locations, a logical partition resulted. A physical partition would exist if more than one server supported the Organization container. Figure 3.16 shows physical partitions for Organization.

In directory systems, all of the entries in a container have to originate from a single physical server. If more than one directory server participates in the container, creating physical partitions, a logical partition must be associated with that physical partition as well. If the container in a directory schema is too generic, it may become too large. Partitioning splits the contents of the container across directory servers. The consequences of this type of partitioning are usually undesirable because it introduces the potential for delays and access problems. On the other hand, a hierarchy that is too detailed impedes access to information and is undesirable as well. As you can see, this process becomes complex and involves trade-offs between being too general and being too specific. As we discussed in the naming section, the simpler the model, the better. The information architecture challenge is arriving at the simplest design that meets the technical and business needs of the organization.

Other Search and Retrieval Issues

Consider the generic container People. Some organizations have discovered that mixing real employee information with information about leased

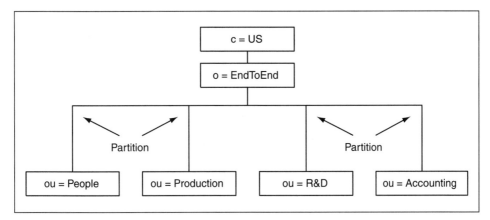

Figure 3.16 Partitions.

employees or contractors represents a legal liability. These organizations have determined that making a logical distinction in directory information pertaining to different types of workers prevents the perception that a contractor is really an employee. They have arbitrarily divided true employees from contract employees in the directory, using distinct containers, objects, and attributes. In addition to limiting legal liability, this design provides a technical benefit as well. Contractor information can reside in an LDAP-enabled security database, while employee information resides in an LDAP-enabled human resources database. Both contractor and employee objects can share a common object type, appear to reside in the same logical directory, yet be maintained in physically separate repositories. Figure 3.17 shows how employee and nonemployee data could be partitioned.

If you attempt to mix information types, you may see similar business or technical implications. It is important to understand the nature of the information that is being managed and to recognize the impact of combining it into common or distinct repositories. These are instances in which a simple design does not support the objectives of the organization.

Application Program Interfaces

Users can access the information in a directory in a variety of ways. The day-to-day user generally relies on an embedded capability in an application, such as an address list search in an e-mail program, to access directory information. In order to develop these applications, application developers

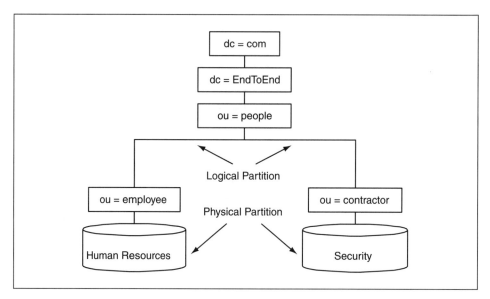

Figure 3.17   Partition example.

use application programming interfaces, or APIs, to access and utilize the directory.

APIs provide thorough and complete access to the capabilities of the directory service. Typical API functions include interfaces to user operations such as read, search, and list, and access to administrative operations, schema discovery, and security. By understanding and using the same set of APIs, application developers benefit from consistent and well-understood service capabilities. Using APIs reduces the cost of application development and maintenance and encourages developers to create more applications that rely on directories.

APIs are available for both X.500 and LDAP implementations. The X.500 API is known as X/Open Group Directory Service (XDS), developed by the XAPI Association. XDS is a "C" language API designed to work with the CCITT 1988 X.500 recommendations. XDS Issue 3 is described in the Open Group Technical Standard C608.

LDAP API is a "C" language API that provides access to directories that comply with LDAP specifications. The LDAP API is defined in RFC-1823.

Management Tools

Vendor-provided directory management capabilities are key differentiators between directory solutions on the market today. Management tools may include text-based as well as graphical interfaces to the directory. Text-based tools are used to automate certain processes or to provide a quicker mechanism to accomplish a given task. Graphical interfaces to the directory that support intuitive and easy-to-use tools reflect the quality of the overall vendor solution.

Some of the capabilities of directory management tools include providing the system manager with the ability to do the following:

- Search for entries or groups of entries based on selected criteria
- Add, modify, and delete directory entries or groups of entries
- Import and export directory information
- Return the directory to a previous state in the event of an error or failure by rolling back directory modifications
- Establish, view, and modify the directory schema, including dynamically restructuring the DIT
- Back up and restore the directory
- Establish the relationships between several physical directories to provide a single logical directory
- Establish information replication between directories
- Monitor directory performance and usage and fine-tune conditions that affect performance
- Establish logging criteria and provide tools to assist with the interpretation of operational logs
- Establish and manage system and directory level access controls for directory information
- Enable various fault tolerance capabilities such as system shadowing and fail-over
- Identify and diagnose system and directory problems and remedy these issues quickly
- Proactively manage the directory to predict and avoid potential error conditions
- Manage multiple physical directories from a single directory management console

Summary

The directory includes a number of integrated components and capabilities to publish and to maintain directory information. The information store provides a repository for the information; the schema, objects, and attributes detail how that information is described, stored, and accessed. The manner in which information is structured has an impact on how easily it can be retrieved. A number of issues affect this, requiring careful analysis and planning to publish the information in a way that meets the needs of the organization.

Naming is a crucial component of an effective directory design. Naming reflects the structure of the directory. Every object in the directory must have a name; the distinguished name of an entry ensures that the object is unique within the naming context. Names should be static, rather than dynamic, and easy to interpret.

CHAPTER

4

Directory Planning

Like any database, a directory out of the box represents a clean sheet of paper. The way that information stored in the directory is represented must be mapped to the business and technical needs and requirements for which the directory will be used. Data structure is intentional; it doesn't happen by accident. One element of planning, then, is the data model or namespace.

Another key element of planning is the distribution of information. Based on the kind of information stored in the directory, the volume of entries, and where and how the information will be used, a strategy must be developed to identify the number and distribution of directory platforms.

One Directory, Many Uses

The directory can serve many purposes in an organization. As we identified in Chapter 1, "Directories and Their Importance to the Enterprise," these purposes fall into several categories:

- Single-purpose directory
- Index, or locator

- Distributed directory
- Meta-directory

These logical distinctions can all be fulfilled using a single logical repository. The distinction is made based on the intended purpose of the directory.

Today, it is pretty common that if you are implementing a directory, your directory is intended to address your specific needs. Depending on where you reside in the organization, your needs may represent very tactical or very strategic requirements. The decision-making process you follow must first address your requirements. It is valuable, however, to examine the impact your implementation will have from an enterprise perspective. For example, deploying a directory that contains much the same information as another directory or database is redundant, leads to inaccuracy, and increases overall costs to the organization from a maintenance, administration, and quality standpoint.

For this reason, it is important to examine the information relationships that the directory represents. By asking the following questions, you will begin to understand that directories do not exist in a vacuum and generally serve more than one requirement. This is why directory service implementations are usually conducted by several teams working toward one common objective. These teams could include Web developers, data, network, or communications management, human resources, or customer service personnel. By pooling requirements and objectives, a shared strategy and general-purpose solution will result. The teams should address the following questions:

- What information will the directory contain?
- Who is the owner of the information?
- Where will the information come from? Does it exist in another database or directory? Can that directory or database satisfy my needs?
- How will the directory be populated? What transformations need to be applied to represent the information correctly? At what frequency will entries be added or changed?
- Who will have access to the information? How will it be used? What is the final disposition of the information? What security or controls need to be applied to ensure that it is used correctly?
- How many entries will exist in the directory? What are our growth expectations, best and worst case?

- What other purposes could the information satisfy? Are initiatives in place to meet these needs? How can we include these in our own initiative?
- Who will manage and maintain the information?

As you think about these questions, you can begin to see how directories can satisfy multiple needs and objectives in an organization. Although it is not uncommon to develop a directory to address a specific requirement like a client list, it is usually more effective to develop a general solution that addresses several requirements. There is no rule that says one directory will satisfy all requirements; however, fewer directories are better than more directories, particularly from the perspective of economies of scale. The cost of maintaining a single, or several, general-purpose directory will be less than maintaining many directories.

Matching Directories to Business Requirements

It is often difficult in a technical community to isolate and identify business requirements. Usually a technical solution comes into existence first and then goes off looking for a business problem to solve. This is the kiss of death, in many cases. Some typical, although not trivial, business requirements that arise in the directory community include the following:

- Presenting one face to the customer
- Making it easier to publish or retrieve information with suppliers, partners, clients, prospects, and so forth
- Reducing the costs of operation and administration
- Facilitating secure correspondence with suppliers, partners, clients, prospects, and so forth
- Improving the speed by which we communicate with suppliers, partners, clients, prospects, and so forth
- Improving the quality of information about suppliers, partners, clients, prospects, competitors, and so forth

From this perspective, the directory must be viewed as a reliable and accessible repository with up-to-date and useful information, eliminating redundant or unproductive activities. A significant challenge, to be sure.

Many tools are available to meet these objectives, and certain communities would argue that data warehousing and similar database technologies meet these needs. So, why use a directory instead? First of all, the directory is optimized for retrieval based on preestablished expectations regarding usage. Second, the directory is usually designed to contain a set of information that is intended to satisfy general information requirements, in a read-only or controlled mode of access. So, although this doesn't preclude the use of database technologies as a repository, ease of access and responsiveness generally indicate that the choice of platform needs to meet these expectations.

As you can see, business requirements that lend themselves to a directory services solution usually have to do with making specific information available to a broad audience, in a flexible yet secure manner. The choice of specific tools to do this is not so important as the protocols and methods used to accomplish this access. Today, the universal language for directory access is the Lightweight Directory Access Protocol (LDAP). Support for LDAP, particularly between enterprises using Internet technologies, will be far more ubiquitous and common than mechanisms like Structured Query Language (SQL) or Open Database Connectivity (ODBC).

Designing the Directory Structure

The most important, time-consuming, and difficult activity related to implementing a directory services solution is the development of the directory namespace. Vendors include many components for developing the namespace. These components are common and accepted ways to represent people, resources, organizations, and locations. More work is being done by standards organizations like the Distributed Management Task Force and the Internet Engineering Task Force and by industry organizations like the Automotive Industry Action Group and the Networked Applications Consortium. This standards development work will reduce the effort required to develop a namespace and to promote interoperability between organizations. It is a rare occasion, though, when standard solutions address all of the needs and requirements of large organizations.

As we stated earlier in this chapter, a directory starts out as a blank sheet of paper. The bad news is that you need to make choices about the way you develop and represent information in the directory. The good news is that these choices will result in a solution that is tailored to the needs of your organization and the extended enterprise.

Getting Started

In the opening sections of this chapter, we identified a number of questions about the information and process requirements that the directory must satisfy. The answers to these questions should provide you with a solid perspective about what needs to be in the directory, who needs to use it, where it should be located, and the like. These are significant issues from a planning perspective. In particular, you should understand the way many different kinds of information will be stored in the directory and the purposes they will satisfy. There is no single "right" way to design a directory. It is an iterative process, consisting of the identification of the content, mapping the content to standard or custom representations, developing the directory structure, evaluating alternatives, and reaching consensus among a broad constituency. It is also important to understand, particularly for those new to the use of the technology, that conducting pilots to examine the feasibility of directory designs is necessary and appropriate. Few directory projects move forward without a false start or two, and testing is a necessary part of the process.

Objects and Attributes

An object is a representation of some real-world entity that we are modeling in the directory. Objects are made up of attributes. Attributes describe the characteristics of the object. Each attribute has a type and a value. For example, the formal definition of the "commonName" attribute in X.520 is as follows:

```
commonName ATTRIBUTE ::= {
SUBTYPE OF        name
WITH SYNTAX           DirectoryString {ub-common-name}
ID        id-at-commonName }.
```

The type of the attribute is a subtype of the super-type "name", used to describe naming attributes. The syntax describes how the information content is represented, and the ID consists of an Object Identifier, or OID, a unique integer value that represents the attribute. An example of an attribute value assertion, or value, might be

```
commonName=Kevin Kampman
```

Object classes represent collections of attributes that can legitimately be used to describe an object. Every directory entry belongs to at least one

object class. For example, the object class Organization Person is described
in X.521 as:

```
person           OBJECT-CLASS            ::= {
     SUBCLASS OF                { top }
     MUST CONTAIN               { commonName | surname }
     MAY CONTAIN                { description |
                                    telephoneNumber |
                                    userPassword |
                                    seeAlso }
     ID                         id-oc-person }
```

Note that the person object class is a subclass of Top, or root of the class
hierarchy, that it must contain either a commonName or surname attribute
value, and optionally, the other attributes listed, such as description, tele-
phoneNumber, userPassword, or seeAlso (an alias reference).

An understanding of the alternatives associated with attributes and objects can be obtained by reviewing the following macro descriptions from
X.501. For attributes, the definition may include the following:

```
ATTRIBUTE MACRO   ::=
BEGIN
TYPENOTATION      ::= AttributeSyntax Multivalued | empty
VALUENOTATION     ::= value (VALUE OBJECT IDENTIFIER)
AttributeSyntax   ::=
"WITH ATTRIBUTE-SYNTAX"  SyntaxChoice
Multivalued                ::= "SINGLE VALUE"
                               |"MULTIVALUE" | empty
SyntaxChoice               ::= value(ATTRIBUTE-SYNTAX)
                      Constraint | type MatchTypes
Constraint          ::= "("ConstraintAlternative")" | empty
ConstraintAlternative ::= StringConstraint | IntegerConstraint
StringConstraint ::= "SIZE" "("SizeConstraint")"
SizeConstraint             ::= SingleValue | Range
SingleValue                 ::= value(INTEGER)
Range                      ::= value(INTEGER) ".." value
                                  (INTEGER)
IntegerConstraint          ::= Range
MatchTypes                 ::= "MATCHES FOR" Matches | empty
Matches                     ::= Match Matches | Match
Match                      ::= "EQUALITY" | "SUBSTRINGS" |
                                  "ORDERING"
END
```

Objects may be defined in the following manner:

```
OBJECT-CLASS MACRO ::=
     BEGIN
```

```
      TYPENOTATION ::=SubclassOf

                                MandatoryAttributes
                                OptionalAttributes
VALUENOTATION ::=
value(VALUE OBJECT IDENTIFIER)
SubclassOf ::=
"SUBCLASS OF" Subclasses |
empty

Subclasses ::= Subclass | subclass ","
          Subclasses
Subclass ::= value (OBJECT-CLASS)
MandatoryAttributes ::=
"MUST CONTAIN {"Attributes"}" | empty
OptionalAttributes ::=
"MAY CONTAIN {"Attributes"}" | empty
Attributes      ::= AttributeTerm | AttributeTerm "," Attributes
AttributeTerm   ::= Attribute | AttributeSet
Attribute       ::= value(ATTRIBUTE)
AttributeSet      ::= value(ATTRIBUTE-SET)
END
```

The X.500 approach for describing objects and attributes has been adopted for use in the IETF in addition to the ITU. It has proven very flexible and effective across all of the directory initiatives, including LDAP. Given this framework for describing objects and attributes, we can now discuss the adoption of standard objects and attributes as well as the development of custom objects and attributes to meet your specific needs.

A key element of the design process is to develop a sense for the kind of information that will be stored in the directory. Most directory projects concentrate on information associated with people and resources in an organization, including roles. For this reason, many of the standard object classes address needs in this area. In the ITU documents X.520 and X.521, standard directory objects and attributes are defined. In the IETF community, standards such as RFC-1274, RFC-2252, and RFC-2256 address standard objects and attributes. The Distributed Management Task Force Common Information Model (CIM) effort also provides definitions for objects and attributes.

With all of these standard alternatives, you might ask, what is the right way to model information in the directory? The answer is, it depends on what you are trying to accomplish. In our experience with large organizations at The Burton Group, very few directory projects settle on just the standard objects and attributes. There are always some elements about the organization and what it is trying to accomplish that require the development of custom objects and attributes. Recognizing this up front is important.

So then, what is the right practice for you? Begin by reviewing the standard objects and attributes that are available, paying particular attention to the syntax and definitions. If an existing attribute or object definition is different from what you intend to use it for, you are better off defining your own custom attribute and object.

Container and Leaf Objects

An object can be either a container of other objects or a leaf object, or node, representing a specific instance of an object. For example, in Figure 4.1 Organization is a container class that could contain multiple instances of Organizational Units.

Inheritance

As you saw in the macro descriptions above, an object class can be unique or it can inherit the characteristics of another, parent class. For example, in Figure 4.2 we show that the object class Person is a subclass of Top. A meaningful example of inheritance is identified in the object class residentialPerson, which is a subclass of Person. A residentialPerson object exhibits all of the characteristics of the Person object class in addition to its own unique characteristics. Therefore, an instance of a residentialPerson object must contain a commonName or surname, plus a localityName.

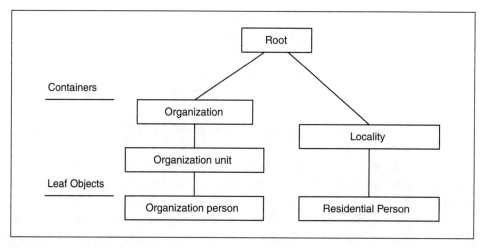

Figure 4.1   Container and leaf objects.

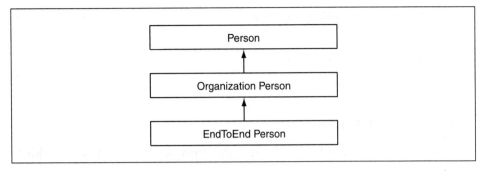

Figure 4.2   Inheritance.

```
residentialPerson        OBJECT-CLASS              ::= {
     SUBCLASS OF              { person }
     MUST CONTAIN        { localityName }
     MAY CONTAIN         { LocaleAttributeSet |
                              PostalAttributeSet |
                              preferredDeliveryMethod |
                              TelecommunicationAttributeSet |
                              businessCategory }
     ID                     id-oc-residentialPerson }
```

Standard Objects

A nonexhaustive list of standard objects from X.521 includes those shown here:

- Country
- Locality
- Organization
- Organizational Unit
- Person
- Organizational Person
- Organizational Role
- Group of Names
- Group of Unique Names
- Residential Person
- Application Process
- Application Entity

- DSA (Directory System Agent)
- Device
- Strong Authentication User
- Certification Authority

Standard Attributes

A nonexhaustive list of standard attributes from X.520 includes those identified here:

LABELING ATTRIBUTES

Name

Common Name

Surname

Given Name

Initials

Generation Qualifier

Unique Identifier

DN (Distinguished Name) Qualifier

Serial Number

GEOGRAPHICAL ATTRIBUTE TYPES

Country Name

Locality Name and Collective Locality Name

State or Province Name

Street Address and Collective Street Address

House Identifier

ORGANIZATIONAL ATTRIBUTE TYPES

Organization Name and Collective Organization Name

Organizational Unit Name and Collective Organizational Unit Name

Title

EXPLANATORY ATTRIBUTE TYPES

Description

Search Guide

Enhanced Search Guide

Business Category

POSTAL ADDRESSING ATTRIBUTE TYPES

Postal Address and Collective Postal Address

Postal Code and Collective Postal Code

Post Office Box and Collective Post Office Box

Physical Delivery Office Name and Collective Physical Delivery Office Name

TELECOMMUNICATIONS ADDRESSING ATTRIBUTE TYPES

Telephone Number and Collective Telephone Number

Telex Number and Collective Telex Number

Teletex Terminal Identifier and Collective Teletex Terminal Identifier

Facsimile Telephone Number and Collective Facsimile Telephone Number

X.121 Address

International ISDN Number and Collective International ISDN Number

Registered Address

Destination Indicator

PREFERENCES ATTRIBUTE TYPES

Preferred Delivery Method

OSI APPLICATION ATTRIBUTE TYPES

Presentation Address

Supported Application Context

Protocol Information

RELATIONAL ATTRIBUTE TYPES

Distinguished Name

Member

Unique Member

Owner

Role Occupant

See Also

The preceding lists of attributes and objects from X.520 and X.521 provide a sense for the kinds of information that the international community feels are common enough to incorporate in a general-purpose directory. Attributes that cover additional requirements, such as your electronic mail address, are defined in other standards, so a careful examination of ongoing directory services standards activities is indicated. Usually, these general components are insufficient to meet the detailed needs of an organization. Using these standard objects and attributes as the basis for your own solution and exploiting the benefits of inheritance, however, will help to ensure some level of compatibility between directory-enabled applications within and between organizations.

Developing Your Own Objects and Attributes

Today, directory services applications usually allow the directory to be extended to include custom objects and attributes. This customization can be accomplished in addition to the industry and standard components that exist and are furnished with most products. This activity should be conducted with some care and with a goal of precision, as users and applications come to rely on the stability of the directory as a mechanism to support other objectives.

It is recommended, but not mandatory, that an organization reserve an object identifier for the organization name. This can be accomplished in the United States by submitting an application to the American National Standards Institute. At the time of this writing, the fee to register an organization is $2500. Once you have obtained the object identifier, you can associate individual attributes and objects to it by extending the numerical OID hierarchy to include them. The OID (in the United States) consists of the following set of numbers: (#.#.#.#.#), where the last number represents your organization. See Figure 4.3 for an explanation of the OID hierarchy. You can then extend the hierarchy by creating an additional hierarchy for attributes and objects. Make sure that you are the only person defining these for your organization and that your work is well publicized and documented within your organization. If a conflict arises with these definitions, you may find yourself performing an unexpected and annoying restructuring of the hierarchy.

```
┌─────────────────────────────────────────────────────────────┐
│   ┌─────────────────────────────────────────────────────┐   │
│   │  "Person" Object Identifier {2.5.6.6}               │   │
│   │                                                      │   │
│   │     2 represents "Joint-ISO-CCITT"                  │   │
│   │     2.5 represents "ds" (directory standards)       │   │
│   │     2.5.6 represents "object-class"                 │   │
│   │     2.5.6.6 represents "object class person"        │   │
│   └─────────────────────────────────────────────────────┘   │
│   ┌─────────────────────────────────────────────────────┐   │
│   │  "Common Name" Attribute Identifier {2.5.4.3}       │   │
│   │                                                      │   │
│   │     2 represents "Joint-ISO-CCITT"                  │   │
│   │     2.5 represents "ds" (directory standards)       │   │
│   │     2.5.4 represents "attribute type"               │   │
│   │     2.5.4.3 represents "attribute type common name" │   │
│   └─────────────────────────────────────────────────────┘   │
└─────────────────────────────────────────────────────────────┘
```

Figure 4.3 Sample ASN.1 object identifiers.

Creation and registration of your own attributes and objects does not ensure compatibility with existing and future applications. Although work is being done in the area of schema discovery so that an application can interpret the information being provided in a directory transaction, this work is incomplete. In addition, there is some overhead associated with schema discovery that may prevent all of the appropriate capabilities from being incorporated into an application. By exploiting the characteristics of inheritance from standard objects, some level of interoperability can be ensured.

The Directory Information Tree (DIT)

The DIT is the structure representing the hierarchy in which the directory content is placed. Another element of the design process is developing this structure to meet the needs of your organization. The DIT is very important as it describes the namespace and the way in which information will be accessed and retrieved from the directory.

A Shallow, Deep, or Rich DIT

When you are designing your DIT, you must consider a number of concerns regarding the top-level view of the information. The first decision is whether the tree will be structured to represent a business view of the organization, a geographical view, or some other perspective, like functional distribution. Because the structure of the directory should be stable and relatively unchanging over time, this is a serious undertaking. The goals are to establish a hierarchy that is as follows:

- Easily searched
- Reasonably shallow (three to five levels deep)
- Can be partitioned (distributed) according the needs of the organization
- Durable or resistant to changes in structure

The perspective you want to model is the one that is most stable. Assess how likely change is from the perspective of geography (does the organization move around a lot?) and from one of organizational structure (does the organization restructure frequently?). If the answer to each of these is yes, a shallow tree may be indicated. In fact, many directory implementations today are being defined by function, to avoid issues associated with geography or structure. Shallow trees, though, are difficult to partition, making it necessary to create and manage large, unwieldy directories requiring high-performance platforms in order to maintain responsiveness.

The following discussion provides a perspective on several top-level approaches to designing the DIT, as shown in Figure 4.4. Early in the development of directories, the CCITT made an assumption that directories would be partitioned by country, using a country/organizational approach. This proved to be unworkable for many organizations, as many of the implementers of directories were multinational corporations. An alternative was attempted that placed the Organization at the root of the hierarchy. While this approach worked for some, for others it failed, as there is no international registration authority for company or organization names that is universally accepted. For organizations that are bounded within one

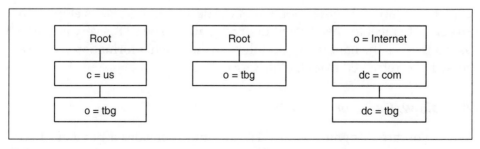

Figure 4.4 Comparison of top-level naming approaches.

nation, or for which national partitioning is not an issue, the country/organization approach is accepted and viable.

Another model that is gaining significant acceptance today is to utilize the approach associated with the Domain Name System (DNS), called Domain Components. Domain Components, or dc, represent the domain elements associated with a platform or entity accessible over the Internet.

For example, if John Smith's e-mail address at End-To-End is jsmith@ endtoend.com, the domain portion of the name is endtoend.com; the domain components are com and endtoend. As shown in Figure 4.5, the domain components are used as the top levels of the hierarchy, and other standard names are used in lower levels of the hierarchy. Using Domain Components as part of the hierarchy works for other top-level domains such as edu, gov, mil, and ec.

The advantage of using DNS is that the naming approach is associated with an internationally recognized body, the IETF, and eliminates the issues associated with international registrations. Domain component naming is not universally supported in all products today but should be generally available during 2000 because it is a basic element of the Microsoft Windows 2000 networking operating system.

Using one of the top-level naming approaches solves the uppermost part of the tree puzzle, and we are only two or three layers deep. The next

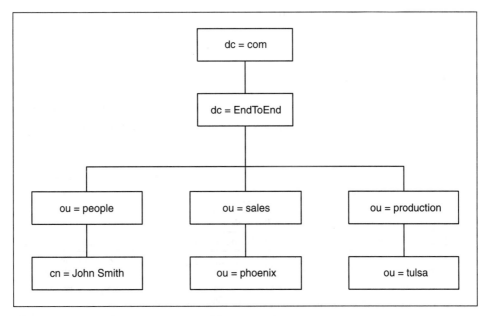

Figure 4.5 Domain Components naming example.

c = us or dc = com			
o = tbg or dc = tbg			
ou = org. unit	ou = location	l = location	ou = location
ou = org. unit	l = location	ou = org. unit	ou = org. unit

Figure 4.6   Combining Organizational Unit and Location.

decision is how best to partition the information beneath the country/organization or domain components: by geography, organizational structure, business or technical function, or a combination of the three. Multiple hierarchy options exist at this level; Figures 4.6 and 4.7 illustrate some alternative approaches to partitioning the information in the directory.

Once the hierarchy is established, other views can be established using aliases, although not all directory products support aliases. In addition, few of those directory implementations include referential integrity for aliases. Referential integrity means that when the entry the alias points to is deleted, the alias or pointer is deleted as well (see Figure 4.8).

Keep in mind that the flatter the tree, the harder it is to partition, or distribute portions of the directory. For large directories or those for which it makes sense to partition the directory by function or application, you may find it necessary to add an arbitrary level to the hierarchy to facilitate splitting the directory.

Distinguished Names

Each branch in the directory hierarchy is represented by a unique name, or a relative distinguished name (RDN). The combination of RDNs that is as-

c = us or dc = com			
o = tbg or dc = tbg			
ou = org. unit	l or ou = location	l or ou = location	ou = function
ou = function (ex. People)		ou = org. unit	ou = function

Figure 4.7   Combining Organizational Unit, Function, and Location.

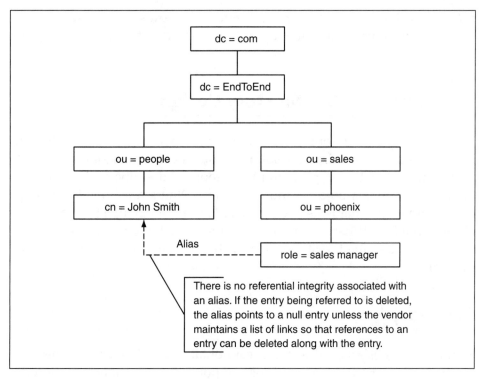

Figure 4.8   Aliases and referential integrity.

sociated with any leaf entry in the directory is known as the Distinguished Name (DN). For example, consider the following directory entry:

dc = com;dc = tbg;ou = consulting;cn = Kevin Kampman

This example shows one container object each for com and tbg, another container object for the Organizational Unit called consulting, and a unique leaf node for the person identified as Kevin Kampman. Com, tbg, consulting, and Kevin Kampman are each RDNs for their respective level in the hierarchy; in combination they represent the DN for the entry. In discussions of uniqueness, the term RDN usually refers to the RDN associated with the leaf entry.

Understanding uniqueness and naming is important because the DN for each entry is often used to represent that entry in other venues, such as aliases and digital certificates. If you need to restructure the tree to accommodate new or different requirements, you may invalidate the DN associated with an entry. In some cases, this will have unintended consequences, such as invalidating digital certificates or alias entries. For this reason, it is important to consider the stability of the directory when you develop the hierarchy.

Implementing the Directory Design

How you implement your directory design depends to a large extent on the capabilities of the directory solution you employ. Some of the products on the market today employ graphical tools to describe and deploy the directory hierarchy, objects, and attributes. Others are built from script files or similar mechanisms like the LDAP Data Interchange Format (LDIF) to build the DIT. Whatever approach is employed, the tools provided enable you to describe the structure and then to enter information into the directory.

Summary

Planning and design for directories cannot take place in a vacuum because the best directory implementations support a true business purpose. A prospective directory may be needed by more than one application or organization, so a team approach that crosses organizational lines may be most effective during the planning stages of directory implementation. It is highly desirable that organizations pool resources and arrive at a shared strategy.

Remember that the design of a directory is an iterative process, and plan for pilot tests of the directory design. Choosing the right hierarchy and naming approach also contributes to the success of your directory implementation. Your vendor selection also influences the detailed design of the directory, so it's important to understand the particular namespace, access protocol, and management characteristics of the directory service you plan to implement.

CHAPTER

5

Directory Technologies

In the short history (30 or so years) of networked computing, specialized directories were developed to address specific needs. Most of these directories concentrated on user, group, and resource administration, password management, address lists, and other similar applications. Directory efforts like X.500 grew out of this tactical morass in an attempt to develop a strategic and platform independent way to manage the same information. Standardization efforts were driven by the desire to collect directory information once and then have the ability to access it from a central point.

The centralized perspective embodied by directories was at odds with distributed or departmental computing. In the mid to late 1980s the proliferation of local area networks and applications such as electronic mail and calendars addressed a compelling issue for departments in organizations. The development of powerful personal computing platforms, along with highly useful applications that helped eliminate the development backlog on host systems, caused organizations to make major investments in desktop platforms. The independence of these platforms was short lived, however. The relatively high cost of peripheral equipment like printers and fixed disks made a case for sharing resources—and the local area network was born.

Initially, local area networks addressed the issue of resource and file sharing. Soon, networked applications gained a foothold in organizations. Departments and groups could send messages to each other, coordinate their schedules, and share applications like databases and spreadsheets. In short, the very technologies that made it possible to break free from corporate computing infrastructures made it possible to recreate a similar infrastructure in a distributed environment. Technical solutions made it possible to interconnect distributed networks back into the corporate systems they tried so hard to break away from. This information distribution model has evolved into client/server and n-tier computing.

Each of these distributed networks has developed its own mechanisms for managing user and resource information. To their chagrin, organizations realized that they were managing the same kind of information at multiple levels in the organization, at the cost of multiple administrative personnel and much redundant data. A lack of standardization across platforms and the inaccuracies associated with multiple points of administration were other issues that emerged in this environment. Security also became a major issue because there was no way to effectively coordinate user access to information and resources. Finally, the cost to the organization in terms of user and administrative productivity became a major concern.

Into this stew of multiple systems, emerging issues, and lack of productivity enters the directory and its potential to alleviate or resolve some of the problems associated with distributed computing. In Chapter 2, "Standards," we briefly introduced two leading areas of directory technology focus, X.500 and LDAP. In this chapter we'll discuss these in more detail, along with a myriad of other solutions that have grown up around directory services and the problems of distributed computing.

The Directory Landscape

In Chapter 1, "Directories and Their Importance to the Enterprise," we mentioned some of the applications that contribute to the directory environment and that directories support. This section is a more thorough examination of what some of these applications are and what role the directory plays in each application.

Host Operating Systems and Applications

Host platforms were initially thought of as the mainframe systems that ran batch or interactive applications like accounting, order entry, customer databases, and payroll. This definition of host platform has expanded to include any shared platform such as a midrange departmental server that hosts local applications. Typically, users access host systems via a terminal or terminal emulation program. Host systems usually require a login and password to the system itself, and perhaps a login and password to the applications that the user accessed. Directories on host systems keep track of security information about users, how they access the system, and what applications they can access. Additionally, directories may provide access to system resources such as print devices and file systems. Individual applications may maintain directory information about the user, including a login and password and profile information. Host applications range from custom systems to office productivity tools like word processing and electronic mail.

Network Operating Systems

When they were first introduced, network operating systems (NOS) utilized a directory to keep track of user account information, including the owner, the owner's manager, the user login and password, when the password expired, and what resources, like disks and printers, a user could access. The directory may contain information about those time periods that a user can access the system and maintain usage information for charge-back purposes. The directory also includes script or profile information that would set up a user environment when the user logged in. In many ways the functions of a NOS directory are direct descendants of the directory applications used on host platforms.

Today, as the integration of distributed network resources like routers, desktops, and servers becomes more universal, the role of the NOS directory has expanded to include information about resources as well as people. Efforts like the Distributed Management Task Force Directory Enabled Networks (DEN) are initiatives to represent devices and other resources under a common umbrella, as elements of a common infrastructure. As the role of the directory broadens, it helps fuel initiatives like software distribution, individualized environments and applications, network quality of service, and routing mechanisms.

NOS-based directories have become both more specialized and more general. They are beginning to provide more specialized capabilities like support for network management. As they become more ubiquitous and serve expanding needs and requirements in the distributed environment, though, they become more general purpose in nature.

Electronic Messaging Systems

Electronic messaging was one of the first applications to realize the potential of networked computing. If you look at the history of electronic messaging vendors, there is a rich field of winners and losers, showing how competitive and important electronic messaging was in the early days of networked computing. From its strong start, electronic messaging has evolved into a comprehensive application.

In order to be considered useful, one of the major requirements a messaging system had to satisfy was ease of locating people and groups on the system. In the infancy of electronic messaging, this requirement often forced a user to type in the name or system ID of the individual or group recipients of the message. Manual entry of names was a crude approach and led to the development of address or pick lists, which provided alphabetized lists of all of the users on the messaging system. Later, messaging systems could synchronize address lists with other systems, so that messages could be transferred between systems. For example, messages could be exchanged between servers on a local area network (LAN) and a mainframe.

Achieving interoperability between messaging systems created the need for directory synchronization between platforms, and it created an industry devoted to address management along with messaging interoperability. The messaging directory synchronization initiative is a significant precursor to the development of today's meta-directory technologies.

Calendar/Scheduling

Group calendar and scheduling applications are similar to messaging systems. A community of users can keep their own schedules on the system and share calendar and scheduling information with others. Calendaring and scheduling systems support a user delegating control of a schedule to another user, restricting or permitting access to events on a schedule, and using the system to coordinate a meeting based on the availability of people and resources. Information about resources like conference rooms may include a profile about the types of facilities available, like the number of chairs, projectors, and telephones. The directory supporting calendaring and messaging systems maintains quite a bit more information about each person or resource than does the directory supporting a messaging system. Calendaring and scheduling systems also require more dynamic information with a higher rate of change than the information maintained in a messaging system. Directories are, however, up to the task of handling calendaring and scheduling systems.

Interoperability between calendar/scheduling systems has been and continues to be a problem. All of the applications in use are proprietary, even though they derive directory information from sources like their host NOS. In the past, working groups have attempted several standards initiatives, including the versit vCalendar specification. The IETF continues standards development work with a standard called iCalendar, which is intended to provide real-time and e-mail-based appointment scheduling.

Remote Access

Remote access solutions provide access to the network to home workers and road warriors. The solutions provide a mechanism to authenticate the user by using a table of entries and passwords. Alternatives to an embedded or application-specific repository are included in remote access solutions that use the RADIUS (Remote Authentication Dial-In User Service, RFC-2138) protocol. When RADIUS is implemented, remote users can be authenticated using a central directory or repository that includes user IDs and passwords.

Collaboration

Collaboration provides a mechanism for sharing information in a structured environment, using a shared information repository for documents, electronic forms, messages, and other correspondence. The information is usually project oriented or corresponds to a common interest. Collaborative applications usually maintain a distinct repository of user and group information. This repository is designed to identify access privileges and other profile information.

Workflow

Workflow applications extend the concept of shared information by introducing the notion of routing works in process. This could be as simple as an approval process for expense requests or as complex as the distribution of application code for testing in a development environment. In either case, processes are defined to manage the distribution of information, responsible parties in the chain of distribution, alternative routes based on availability or time sensitivity, and the status or state of the work being performed. The directory is used to identify objects, participants, capabilities, roles, and relationships and to provide suspense tracking for information in the workflow process.

Facsimile

Networked facsimile solutions can be standalone or integrated with applications like electronic messaging systems. Facsimile is considered another delivery mechanism for messages and information. This information may be distributed to individuals or groups, using single requests or broadcasts, in either a push or pull mode. The directory is used to identify the delivery mechanism, such as telephone or network, associated with the recipient, and other profile information.

Conferencing Systems

Several conferencing domains are in use in industry today that use video, data, and voice technologies individually or in combination. Directories play a role in conferencing by identifying information about participants or groups of participants and the ways in which they can be reached or connected to the conference. Users can develop profiles for identifying the capabilities of the resources being used. A directory can provide or support authentication mechanisms for the conferencing systems.

Document Management

Document management solutions provide a mechanism to store and access information from a centralized repository. The systems provide version and access control, as well as status information, such as who has the document checked out of the system, when it should be purged, and if it is in an editable or read-only form. The directory plays a role in document management systems by maintaining object, owner, management, and user profiles.

Other Directories

A wide range of other directories is in use in the enterprise, some of which contain, share, or rely on the same information. These directories include

Human Resources applications, physical plant security systems, Enterprise Resource Planning systems, project management, telephone and PBX systems, real estate or property management, accounting and payroll systems, customer databases, contact management systems, Public Key Infrastructure, and others too numerous to name. Potential redundancies, overlaps, and opportunities for integration exist among all of these directories; be aware that directories lurk in a multitude of locations within the enterprise.

Directory Technologies

Chapter 2 presented a discussion of the standards associated with directories. This section presents some of the implementations of these standards.

X.500

In Chapter 2 we discussed the X.500 standard as one of the seminal influences on the state of today's directory services solutions. In fact, it is either the core engine or the model for many of today's commercial offerings. Over the years, industry consultants have characterized the directories that implement the best features of X.500 as "X.500-like." Even though there are solutions that have no relationship to X.500 at all, any directory that has an LDAP interface shares some of the characteristics of the X.500 naming hierarchy.

Although X.500 has not been widely adopted as a standalone directory service technology, it is a common application inside of many commercial directory service applications. For example, in several of today's meta-directory product offerings, X.500 is the information repository. Vendors such as Control Data Systems, ICL, Isocor, Isode, and others have developed commercial X.500 products.

Distributed Computing Environment (DCE)

Although not in widespread use, the Open Software Foundation DCE model is an example of an environment that makes significant use of directory services capabilities. A DCE environment consists of one or more cells, or units of operation and administration. A cell is a group of users, systems, and resources sharing a common purpose and services.

From a directory perspective, two major components of DCE are of interest: the Global Directory Service (GDS) and the Cell Directory Service

(CDS). The Global Directory Service supports the global naming environment inside of cells and between cells. It is based on X.500, and it is used to locate DCE resources that do not reside in the local cell. The Domain Name System (DNS) can be used in place of the GDS. The Cell Directory Service, on the other hand, is responsible for storing and maintaining names of local resources in the cell. It also maintains access control lists for each resource in the cell. The CDS can be distributed, or replicated, across multiple platforms within the cell.

LDAP

The Lightweight Directory Access Protocol is the industry standard for accessing directory information. Due to its widespread commercial acceptance, LDAP is seen as the integration solution, or directory glue, that makes it possible to access and manage directories with an LDAP interface, regardless of the native architecture or protocols. As we described in Chapter 2, the LDAP standards describe a protocol, a data interchange format, and an Application Program Interface. LDAP relies on the same hierarchical information model as X.500 does. Information can be imported or exported from the directory using the LDAP Data Interchange Format (LDIF). LDIF is text based and consists of blocks of entry information.

LDAP does have its shortcomings. Certain key features, such as access control and replication, are missing from the current version, LDAP v 3. The directory community has raised interoperability between vendors as an issue. The formation of the Directory Interoperability Forum in the summer of 1999 offers promise as vendors work to resolve issues with the standard.

Internet-Related Technologies

A number of Internet solutions include or make use of directory services capabilities. This section describes the most common of these Internet solutions.

Dynamic Host Configuration Protocol (DHCP)

The Dynamic Host Configuration Protocol is a protocol used to assign IP addresses to computers on a request basis. A DHCP server maintains a pool of available IP addresses. When it receives a request from a DHCP client, it provides an address, the subnet mask, and optional information like the addresses of a DNS server, default gateway, and other services to the client. DHCP simplifies address management on client workstations and makes better use of a limited IP address space, as these are returned to the pool once the address is "given up" by the DHCP client. Even though DHCP doesn't require the use of a directory service, and most implementations utilize a flat file or database, for this information, DHCP does contribute information to other directories and is a candidate technology for the use of a common directory when initiatives like DEN become more common.

Domain Name System (DNS)

The Domain Name System is a specialized directory that provides name-to-address mapping for network resources. DNS is a database that is distributed globally across the Internet. The DNS database is a client/server database, consisting of name servers and resolvers, or clients. The client resolver is usually embedded in network clients, and it enables network clients to locate network resources. For example, in a browser, terminal emulator, or file transfer program, when you type the logical name of a site, such as www.tbg.com, the DNS server will return the numeric address or other information currently associated with that site (nn.nn.nn.nn) to the resolver. An example of a resolver application is nslookup.

DNS is constructed and distributed hierarchically, with parent and children nodes. At the top, there is a root entry. Beneath the root, DNS is partitioned into top-level domains, such as .com, .edu, .gov, and .mil. The top-level domains are managed by the Internet Network Information Center (InterNIC). Each of the top-level domains are partitioned into nodes, or components, of the overall database. Each node can be further partitioned into subdomains. Management of the nodes is accomplished at that level and by its subdomains.

Every domain is labeled with a name that identifies it relative to its parent domain. The full domain name is the complete sequence of labels, separated by periods, from the leaf domain to the root, or Top. For example, a server at The Burton Group might be called *testbed.oh.tbg.com.* The intent of this hierarchy is to ensure unique naming for host platforms on the Internet to accomplish the logical-to-physical name mapping. The most common implementation of DNS is the Berkley Internet Name Domain (BIND), which is now maintained by the Internet Software Consortium.

Name Servers

DNS has several types of information servers, or hosts. These information servers are known as *name servers.* A name server is responsible for managing all of the information for a component of the namespace. These managed components are known as zones. The name server is considered the authority for its zone. It may also be the authority for other zones.

A primary master name server collects all of the information that is maintained in its zone locally from the server that supports it. A secondary master name server gets the information it keeps in its database from another authoritative server for the zone. The process of collecting this information is known as a zone transfer. Having multiple name servers distributes the load and provides redundancy should one of the servers become unavailable.

Most of the real capabilities for responding to queries reside in the name servers. When a resolver running on a client computer issues a query for an IP address or a host name on behalf of a user or an application, name servers are able to collect and return information about resources other than those they manage. They are capable of searching through the namespace for information. This is known as name resolution.

Name servers conduct two kinds of queries: the recursive query and the iterative, or nonrecursive, query. In a recursive query, a name server accepts the responsibility to respond to a resolver by issuing additional queries based on the knowledge gained to resolve the request, until the query is satisfied or the information is determined not to be available. In an iterative query, the name server merely responds with the information it knows to the resolver. The resolver then uses this information to issue additional requests, iteratively, until it finds the desired information.

Name Mapping

Internet names consist of a logical and a physical address. For the server www.tbg.com, this is 199.104.68.66. Each of these addresses is hierarchical. Figure 5.1 shows these from the least specific to the most specific components. Note that to show the correspondence, the order of the logical ad-

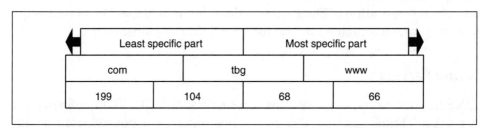

Figure 5.1   Name mapping.

dress is reversed. This is because the DNS is organized in order to resolve information from the least to most specific component.

Records

Information in the DNS database is represented in several kinds of records. These records serve multiple purposes, providing flexibility and increased capabilities. The purpose of certain DNS records is described in Table 5.1.

Dynamic DNS (DDNS)

Dynamic DNS provides real-time incremental updates of DHCP address assignments to DNS servers. Until DHCP and DDNS were implemented, the DNS zone information was maintained in static tables that had to be updated manually. DDNS takes advantage of DHCP by assigning changes on-the-fly, as it is notified of changes. This ensures that the correct IP address is assigned to the correct host name. One of the most effective ways to implement this is to use a common, distributed directory to support the DDNS server.

Network Information Service (NIS)

Network Information Service provides a centralized, platform-independent management database in a distributed computing environment. It can

Table 5.1   DNS Record Types

A	Provides the logical name to physical address mapping
CNAME	Provides the canonical name, for alias resolution
HINFO	Provides information about hosts
MX	Identifies mail exchange records, for prioritization and failover of mail delivery
NS	Identifies the name server for the domain
PTR	Provides a physical address to logical name mapping
SOA	Identifies the authority for this domain data
SRV	Identifies service or capability mappings
TXT	Identifies text based information
WKS	Provides information about well-known services

contain information such as host tables and password management files, and it is designed to streamline system administration across multiple platforms by centralizing shared information into a single repository that is distributed across the network.

NIS is built on the client/server model. An NIS server contains NIS data files, or maps. NIS clients request information contained in the maps from an NIS server. There are two kinds of NIS servers, masters and slaves. A master is the authoritative source for map information and is responsible for distribution to slave servers. Slave servers represent read-only repositories for map information and respond to client requests. Master servers may also respond to client requests, but slave servers help to provide information and load distribution.

ph

ph is an application that returns information about people from a ph directory server. Originally developed at the University of Illinois, ph is a telephone directory lookup command that returns name, address, telephone number, and e-mail address from the server. ph is currently described in RFC-2738.

whois

whois is a directory service designed to locate resources, people, and organizations, primarily on the Internet. In the early days of the Internet, it was implemented on a centralized basis, but it soon outgrew this approach. Today, it is implemented locally by businesses and educational institutions, as well as nationally by organizations like Network Solutions, Inc. RFC-2167 describes RWHOIS, a hierarchical and scalable enhancement to WHOIS based on DNS, X.500, and other Internet protocols, like the Simple Mail Transfer Protocol.

Network and Host Operating System Directory Implementations

A number of embedded, application-specific directories are in use today. The following descriptions provide a high-level survey of some of the more common implementations of directories in network and host operating systems.

Novell Directory Services (NDS)

Novell is the network operating system vendor that developed the highly successful NetWare network operating system. In its early versions, NetWare utilized localized repositories for account and resource management called the Bindery. Users authenticated to the Bindery on their preferred, or home, server, which held their account information and profiles, in addition to resource management information for that platform. Servers communicated with each other regarding access rights and privileges using Bindery information. This information was tied very closely to the local platform, which limited its scalability.

The NetWare Bindery was considered a de facto directory standard in the application development community. Applications that included a directory were able to pull user information from the NetWare Bindery to populate the directory. There was little real integration, however, between applications and the NOS, feeding the early interest in tools to conduct directory synchronization.

Starting with version 4 of NetWare, Novell loosened this coupling of user and resource information to specific platforms. Novell Directory Services is a network-wide, distributed repository that contains information associated with users and resources.

NDS is loosely based on the X.500 object model, but it does not incorporate underlying X.500 protocols like DAP or DSP. Because NDS was originally closely tied to the underlying operating system, Novell developed its own access and information sharing application program interfaces and protocols instead of relying on standards. Standards-based external client and programmatic access to this information is provided by LDAP. NDS has evolved into a multi-platform enterprise directory service.

Banyan StreetTalk

Banyan's StreetTalk is the naming and directory services component of the Banyan Virtual Networking System (VINES) network operating system. Banyan also developed a version of StreetTalk as a directory service for Windows NT.

StreetTalk is used to identify and manage network components across the network. These components include users and resources. Resources include services, lists, and servers. Each element of the name service is called an item. Items are associated with groups, which are, in turn, associated with an organization.

StreetTalk is a distributed database. It is distributed across all of the servers in the VINES network, so that the naming service functions even if a server is unavailable. User and group information is associated with and maintained on a physical server, while organizational information is virtual. That is, it has no association with a particular component of the network. The distribution of user, group, and organizational information is transparent to the end user, so that all resources appear as components on the network, rather than being associated with a particular platform or device.

Microsoft Windows NT Advanced Server and Active Directory

Microsoft entered the client/server NOS arena in a joint effort with IBM in the late 1980s. The result of the joint effort was known as OS/2 LAN Manager. At the same time, Microsoft began embedding peer networking services on the desktop with a version of Windows called Windows for Workgroups. OS/2 LAN Manager differed from its competition because the NOS functioned as an application that ran on top of the operating system, rather than as an integral component of the operating system.

When the IBM/Microsoft partnership fell apart, Microsoft developed an integrated operating system and NOS called Windows NT Advanced Server (NTAS). NTAS provides a graphical user interface to manage the network and a directory to manage users and servers. NTAS is also an application server, hosting capabilities such as a messaging system (Exchange Server) and a database (SQL Server).

An NTAS network is structured using a domain model. Domains are a mechanism for partitioning the network into logical management units, for both account and resource management. Domains are viewed logically as separate entities. Trust relationships can be established in order to allow resources in one domain to access resources in another domain, and to tie together administration of the domains.

Within each domain, domain controllers are installed on servers. The Primary Domain Controller (PDC) holds the directory, also known as the Security Accounts Manager database. All changes to the directory in the domain are conducted on the PDC. Changes are replicated to synchronized copies of the directory maintained on Backup Domain Controllers (BDC). BDCs provide redundancy and load balancing capabilities, and they can be promoted to the role of PDC if the primary server goes down.

The NTAS directory is similar to the Novell Netware Bindery because it is used to manage information about user accounts, groups, and networked resources. It provides some of the capabilities of Banyan StreetTalk because it begins to abstract the relationship of an account separately from a particular server. The user logs into a domain, not a particular server, and has access to resources in other domains based on security relationships. The directory, though, is still very much a part of the NOS for which it was designed.

The information in the directory is accessible to other applications. Microsoft Exchange and Lotus Notes are examples of a messaging and a collaboration application that both use the information in the NTAS directory to populate their own directories.

With the release of Windows 2000, Microsoft incorporates a global directory service called Active Directory into the NOS. Comparable to Novell's NDS, this enterprise directory provides an object-based management store for users and resources, with standards-based access mechanisms for users and applications. Active Directory is a distributed directory, and it supports locating resources in the enterprise using a global catalog. It provides granular access control to distribute administrative responsibilities. Active Directory supports a number of security standards, including Kerberos and public-key mechanisms for authentication. It is closely coupled to the Domain Name System, with direct mapping to DNS naming, and it also supports Dynamic DNS. The directory is extensible and supports the creation and inclusion of new objects and attributes.

Microsoft Exchange Server

The Microsoft Exchange Server has a directory service for managing objects patterned after the X.500 standard. These objects include users and resources like mailboxes, distribution lists, public folders, and other Exchange servers. The directory has integrated support for LDAP protocol access to directory information.

Lotus Notes/Domino Server

Lotus also has an embedded X.500-based directory service. Notes/Domino is a vendor-independent application that runs on Microsoft NT, Unix, AS/400, and OS/390. Because the Notes/Domino application operates independently from the underlying server environment, its directory service maintains its own information about objects like people and groups. The Notes/Domino directory also uses a certificate-based authentication mechanism that provides X.509 version 3 compatibility. Notes/Domino also supports LDAP access.

Legacy Environments

In the world of the mainframe, minicomputer, and the workstation, operating systems like IBM's OS/390 and AS/400, various flavors of Unix, and Compaq/Digital's OpenVMS are common for enterprise systems. These operating systems were first designed to support terminal access to the host. Organizational moves to intelligent desktop platforms and the deployment of networks and protocols like TCP/IP have changed this access paradigm, but the heavy-duty processing roles and capabilities of these platforms remain the same. Like application systems, the role of a directory in these operating systems is to provide security, authentication, and access to system resources. The account directories on legacy systems, however, provide little in the way of direct publishing capabilities or shared information outside of their native environment.

In the Unix environment, for example, native account management information is kept in files like passwd (password) and group. The information kept in these files is very rudimentary and platform specific; it includes the information shown in Figure 5.2 and Figure 5.3. The files are usually maintained using Unix administration shells, such as adminsh. Figure 5.2 shows an example based on password, and Figure 5.3 shows an example based on group.

Another example of an integrated account information management platform is the IBM security environment called Resource Access Control

/etc/passwd example:

Attribute	Value	Meaning
login-name	kkampman	User's system login identification
Encrypted-password	@3e7d%n#i2U	User's password, encrypted for security
user-ID	102	System assigned numeric ID
group-ID	100	Administrator assigned group ID
Info	Kevin Kampman	Logical name
Directory	/usr/kkampman	Home directory at login
Program	/bin/sh	Operating system shell at login

Figure 5.2   Password example.

/etc/group example:

Attribute	Value	Meaning
group-name	authors	Group identification
Encrypted-password	Zx5r6^1Tio9b	Group password, if assigned
group-ID	100	System assigned numeric ID
login-name-list	kkampman, tkampman	Group membership

Figure 5.3 Group example.

Facility (RACF). This database mechanism provides a way to authenticate users, control their access to system resources, and log their activities. Compaq/Digital OpenVMS uses a System User Authorization file (SYSUAF) to provide similar functionality.

Summary

In the world of networked computing, a number of directory repositories serve the needs of specific functions or applications or play a general-purpose role. Starting with host operating systems, these repositories were implemented to contain information about people and services within the environment. As client/server and distributed systems became more prevalent, the nature of the directory changed as well. Today, these directory repositories are becoming general purpose, whether they are embedded in the operating system or in application systems. As we will see, the competition for the directory space is becoming intense. As the use of directories grows, so will the need for interoperability.

CHAPTER

6

Security

Security solutions address four major requirements for conducting business electronically: identifying an entity, or *authentication*; protecting the contents of an electronic transaction, or *confidentiality*; ensuring that the contents are what the originator sent, or *integrity*; and preventing the sender from disputing the transaction after it is sent, or *nonrepudiation*. Cryptographic techniques, used in conjunction with directory information, address these requirements.

In this chapter we examine some of the inner workings of security and directory services and the role of the directory in security. We discuss common cryptographic techniques and how directory services support capabilities like authentication and encryption for security approaches such as tunneling protocols. Chapter 7, "Network Management," discusses how the cryptographic techniques discussed in this chapter are used to support security-related techniques in network management.

Security Overview

Security is essentially the management of risk. The cost of implementing security should not exceed the value of the information being protected; therefore, some measure of value or sensitivity needs to be applied to each situation. Assets such as intellectual property should be categorized according to both their value and the risk their disclosure would represent to the organization.

As a first step in the development of any solution, an organization needs to address its security requirements. Too often, organizations consider networked computer security as an activity that is secondary to development, or they implement security only by postimplementation audits and recommendations. Development organizations often view a security officer as a necessary evil, someone who passes judgment without being involved in the decision-making process. While segregation of responsibility has its purpose, in today's environment, security is too important an issue to be relegated to the periphery of network design. Security is an integral part of any architecture, design, or implementation, and all participants and contributors must acknowledge its importance by planning for it before the network is implemented.

A security framework that identifies boundaries for information may be structured to represent a range from *public*, to *sensitive*, to *never to be disclosed*. For example, a company might use a color model, from green, to yellow, to red, to represent public, sensitive, and never to be disclosed. The same levels of security should also correspond to the personnel who can access the information under consideration. And it's not just employees of a company who need to be categorized—external entities such as the public, business partners, or dealers might also have different privileges for working with company information.

A network security model, such as the one shown in Figure 6.1, should incorporate a boundary model that provides a similar method for the segregation of information. Certain information should never be available on or transmitted over a network, without careful scrutiny, such as the private-key component of a public/private key pair. Other information may be located on secure platforms to which only selected individuals have access, and some information may be encrypted when transmitted. Still other information may be public, and the organization may make special efforts to attract attention to it. Whatever the information represents, the underlying infrastructure and capabilities of the network and application infrastructure should serve to present or isolate it, depending on its sensitivity.

A number of publications discuss information protection. One of the most comprehensive series of publications is the National Security Agency's Rainbow Series, which can be found at www.radium.ncsc.mil/tpep/library/rainbow/. The book *Computer Security* by Dieter Gollman (Wiley, 1999) provides a structured overview of the security environment and issues pertinent to a security strategy.

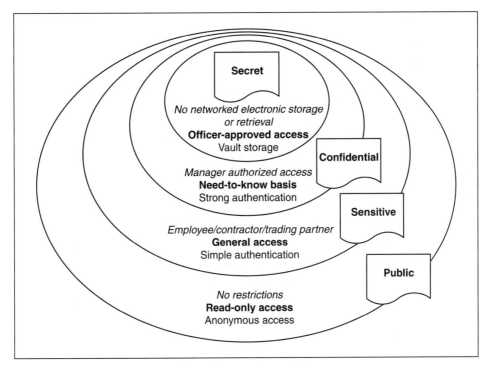

Figure 6.1   Information sensitivity and protection policies.

Security Concepts

Before we discuss the many aspects of security that rely on directories, let's review a few critical security concepts.

Access Control

Access control represents the range of user capability, or permissions, associated with an object. For example, in the Unix operating system, file system objects have read, write, or execute permissions associated with the owner of the object, a group, or the world (everyone). In a directory, access controls are associated with directory entries and domains, restricting or allowing actions such as compare, read, add, remove, modify, import, and export to a user or group. In a network environment, access controls identify what resources, such as an application, service, or file system, are available to particular users or groups of users. Time restrictions, for example, may also be designated by access controls.

Authentication

Authentication is the process of verifying identity, that is, proving that users or resources are who they say they are. Authentication exists in levels ranging from *simple* to *strong*.

Simple authentication is based on the knowledge of a paired set of information that includes a name or identifier and a password. Systems using simple authentication assume that if someone asserting an identity knows the password associated with an identifier, the user is that person or resource. Simple authentication usually involves passing the name and password pair in cleartext over the network. In today's environment, simple authentication is fraught with the dangers associated with the compromise of passwords at the source, on servers, as well as by the possibility that the information could be captured during its transmission. Simple authentication is also known as *single-factor authentication.*

Strong authentication is the use of some form of encryption to prevent authentication information from being compromised. For example, in Kerberos, a shared secret, embodied in an encryption key, is associated with every principal, or client, that accesses the authorization server. A user enters a password on the client to initiate a session request with the authorization server. The client does not send the password over the network; instead, it sends a simple request for client authentication to the server. The response from the server, and every part of the correspondence thereafter, is encrypted, using the client's key, the server key, the session key, or a specially generated encryption key, depending on the transaction type. Kerberos is a component of most Distributed Computing Environment implementations today, and it is included in Windows 2000.

Strong authentication is a response to an additional requirement in network security: that someone else monitoring the transactions cannot impersonate the client. Although all of the transactions in strong authentication are encrypted, the case can be made that the authenticator can impersonate the client due to the knowledge it possesses. For this reason, the authentication mechanism must be physically and logically secured from compromise.

Strong authentication depends on *two-factor authentication.* Two-factor authentication requires that at least two of the following three conditions be present and correctly associated with the user:

- Something the user has, such as a token or smart card

- Something the user knows, such as a password or personal identification number (PIN)

- Something unique about the user, such as fingerprints, voice prints, or retinal scans

You probably encounter many examples of strong authentication in your everyday life. If you use an automatic teller machine, it requires the use of a bank card and PIN, which are two authentication factors. Debit cards, smart cards, and randomizing token cards all require the entry of a PIN, again for two-factor authentication.

Biometrics, or the use of unique aspects of a user's body, can be used as a replacement for a PIN in two-factor authentication. Two applications of biometrics are obtaining fingerprints at the entrance to theme parks and retinal scans at automatic teller machines.

Simple and strong authentication methods take many forms in security implementations. The distinctions between them fall on a continuum rather than being strictly differentiated. Even within strong authentication methods, some methods are stronger than others.

Digital Certificates

Public-key cryptography is based on a mathematical algorithm that ensures that anything encrypted using a public key can be decrypted using the private key associated with the public key. Conversely, anything encrypted using the private key can be decrypted using the public key. The encryption algorithms used are one way. One-way encryption means that once information is passed through the algorithm using one of the keys, the information can be read only by the holder of the matching key.

A digital certificate is an affirmation that the public key embodied in the digital certificate is bound to the identity of the specific individual or organization using the same digital certificate. A third party, a certificate authority, creates and signs the digital certificate. The certificate authority provides assurance that certain conditions have been met that verify the identity of the digital certificate holder. The public key carried in the certificate corresponds to a private key that is held by the certified entity. The digital certificate contains other information such as the conditions under which the certificate is valid and an expiration date.

Digital certificates are used to create *digital signatures.* Digital signatures certify that the person who originated the document is the one who holds the private key associated with that digital certificate.

Security and Directories

It is important to remember that, by itself, the directory is not a security mechanism. The directory can, however, play an important role in providing security within a network because it can serve as a repository for security information used to identify and control entities throughout the network. These entities can be both users and devices.

If a directory is used to support security, the architecture of the directory itself must take security into consideration. The directory architecture should identify the following:

- Where security information is located in the directory schema, so that access controls can be targeted to the right information

- How the directory server is secured, both physically and logically

- Those applications permitted to access directory information

- The conditions under which directory information can be accessed

When directories are used to maintain security information, a particularly critical concern is that security requirements should be in place to prevent the compromise of sensitive information stored within the directory. Why does information associated with the directory itself need to be protected? Let's consider an example. Digital certificate management applications specify roles and responsibilities associated with certificate generation, assignment, and revocation. When certificates are stored in the directory, certain permissions are associated with these roles to ensure the viability of the information. Unauthorized access to the keys used to generate certificates could compromise the certificate authority and force the revocation of all the certificates issued by the authority. As you can see, special care must be taken to manage information associated with the certificates as well as the certificates themselves, and the design of a directory must take these considerations into account.

Using directories to maintain security information provides several advantages. The development of an application is simplified when security information is maintained in a directory because functions associated with security can be accessed using the directory service. With one repository for security rather than a repository for each application, the information is actually more secure. A single repository eliminates duplicate entries for one entity, making the control and management of security information much easier.

Security Standards and Directories

Various standards-setting organizations have a number of security standards in use and other candidates for standards in development. The standards include Kerberos and IPSec, as well as Secure Sockets Layer/

Transport Layer Security (SSL/TLS), Secure WAN for networks, Secure Multipurpose Internet Message Extensions (S/MIME), Secure HTTP for Web browsers, and Secure Electronic Transactions (SET) for credit card payments. Each of these standards incorporates cryptography as a core element for the protection of information. The standards community is focusing considerable attention on the use of key and certificate information associated with cryptography.

Other ongoing standards work sponsored by the IETF includes encryption (Open Specification for Pretty Good Privacy), several authentication efforts (Authenticated Firewall Traversal, Common Authentication Technology, and One-time Password Authentication), and digital certificate-related activities (Public Key Infrastructure [X.509], Simple PKI, and XML Digital Signature). These efforts are in response to the need to protect information in today's globally networked environment.

Even though some of the standards associated with directories describe an authentication mechanism, they address only how the directory stores authentication information and how this information should be used. Protocols like the Lightweight Directory Access Protocol (LDAP) and Directory Access Protocol (DAP) are not in themselves secure, and they should be considered only communications components in an overall security architecture.

X.509: The Directory as an Authentication Framework

The ITU recommendation, X.509, identifies how authentication information, specifically digital certificates, should be created and published in a directory. X.509 identifies the form of authentication information to be placed in the directory, how the information is created and placed in the directory, and how the information can be retrieved. X.509 is one of the few X.500 series of recommendations that is almost universally accepted. It is recognized as the standard for publishing digital certificates and is supported by all directory services and Public Key Infrastructure (PKI) vendors.

Overview of Cryptographic Techniques

We have already mentioned that directories are often used to store information about digital certificates. To better understand the application of directories to digital certificates and other applications that rely on cryptography, this section presents some basic information about cryptography and cryptographic techniques used in networked computing.

Trust in the networking world is the agreement between two parties that they will interact. Trust also describes the technical conditions surrounding these interactions. In this section we give you a broad overview of how cryptography using public/private keys and other techniques can be applied to address four trust requirements:

Authentication. The verification that an entity truly represents who it purports to be.

Confidentiality. The protection of the content of some correspondence from unintended or unauthorized use, accomplished using encryption.

Integrity. The provision of a mechanism to ensure that the content of some form of correspondence has not been altered over the course of a transmission. It is usually accomplished in the digital world by generating a mathematically unique value, a hash, by passing the content through an algorithm designed for this purpose. Then the hash is signed digitally by the originator. This binds the content to the hash and the hash to the originator.

Nonrepudiation. The assurance that once a transmission of correspondence is delivered to its intended recipient, the originator cannot later deny the authenticity of the correspondence that was sent.

To support these trust requirements, security services apply one of the following three cryptographic techniques:

- Digital signatures
- Encryption
- Hashing

Table 6.1 identifies the relationship between trust and the techniques used to ensure trust. The primary approaches used to support trust requirements are cryptographic techniques.

Cryptographic Techniques

Before discussing how cryptographic techniques support trust, here's a brief overview of each cryptographic technique.

Table 6.1 Trust Requirements and Associated Techniques

REQUIREMENT	TECHNIQUES
Authentication	Digital signature
Confidentiality	Encryption
Integrity	Signed hash
Nonrepudiation	Encryption or signed hash, digital signature, time stamping

Digital Signatures

A digital signature represents that the only entity that could have signed the correspondence is one that holds the private-key component of the public/private key pair. A public/private key is an application of an *asymmetric* cryptographic algorithm. An algorithm is asymmetric when one key is used to encrypt the data and a separate, but mathematically related, key is used to decrypt the data. Figure 6.2 shows the process used in encryption with asymmetric algorithms.

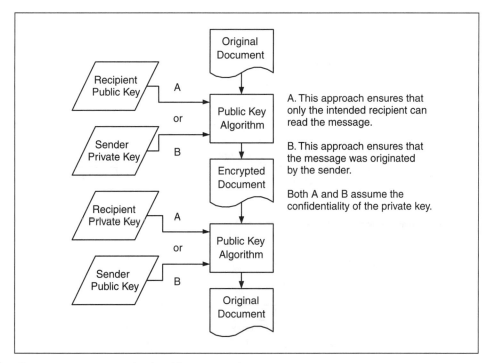

Figure 6.2 Asymmetric algorithm processing.

Digital signatures do have a limitation because the private key can be compromised.

Encryption

Encryption is accomplished by passing the content of the correspondence through a mathematical algorithm, which uses an encryption key to encrypt the data. With public/private keys, one of the keys is used to encrypt the data; the other key is needed to decrypt the data. Other algorithms use a single key to encrypt and decrypt the data; these algorithms are known as *symmetric* algorithms. Figure 6.3 shows the process used in encryption with symmetric algorithms.

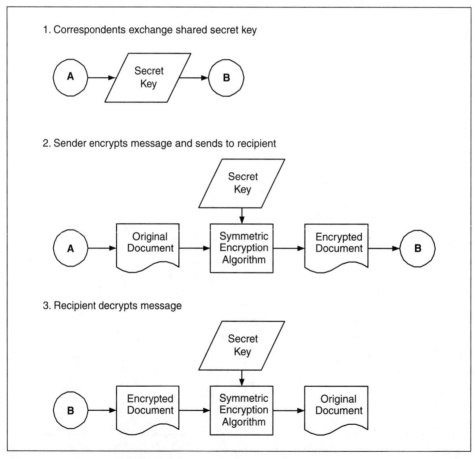

Figure 6.3 Symmetric algorithm processing.

Single-key algorithms are faster and require fewer computational resources. Often, a single-key technique is used to encrypt the data, and then the key itself is encrypted using the public/private key algorithm. This approach is more efficient overall.

Signed Hash

Passing information through a special program that creates a mathematical value results in a hash value. The algorithm that produces the mathematical result is designed to generate a value that can be associated with only the original information content. Signing the hash is accomplished using the digital signature of the originator to verify that the hash value is associated with the correspondence.

The hash value indicates that the content of the document is the original. The hash value is the result of passing the contents through a computation that generates a unique value that only the contents could generate. The digital signature, applied to the hash, indicates that the hash was generated by the signer.

Cryptographic Algorithms

Digital signature, encryption, and signed hash all use specific algorithms, or methods to accomplish their role in security. An entire series of algorithms has been developed to address these needs. We have included just a selected set of these algorithms and standards here:

DES. Data Encryption Standard, or Data Encryption Algorithm. A recognized federal standard in use since 1976 for all unclassified government communications. DES encrypts data in 64-bit blocks, an approach called a block cipher. It is a symmetric algorithm because it uses the same 56-bit key to encrypt and to decrypt the data.

Triple-DES. A variant of DES that encrypts the information serially three times with three separate keys.

DSS. Digital Signature Standard, developed by the U.S. government. The standard defines a public-key cryptographic system for generating and verifying digital signatures.

Diffie-Hellman. The Diffie-Hellman algorithm is useful for distributing keys, but it cannot be used to encrypt or decrypt messages. Diffie-Hellman was the first public-key algorithm. It is a component of the IETF's Internet Security Association/Key Management Protocol (ISAKMP).

IDEA. International Data Encryption Algorithm. Like DES, IDEA is also a block cipher. It operates on 64-bit blocks, using a 128-bit key. The same key is used for encryption and decryption.

MD5. Message Digest 5, a one-way hash function that produces a 128-bit hash. Ron Rivest developed MD5 in 1991. Message digests are used to compress a document into a single figure before the figure is signed with a private key.

RSA. Named for the developers, Ron Rivest, Adi Shamir, and Leonard Adelman, and patented in 1983, RSA is the most commonly used public-key algorithm and is considered the de facto standard for public-key algorithms.

RC2. Rivest Cipher 2 is a variable key sized encryption algorithm that uses a 64-bit block. It is a proprietary algorithm owned by RSA Data Security, Inc. It is intended to replace DES, although the algorithm was published in 1997. It can use either a 40-bit or 128-bit key.

RC4. Rivest Cipher 4 is a variable key sized encryption algorithm that is considered secure. The algorithm is owned by RSA Data Security, Inc. It has been published for scrutiny and is widely used in applications such as Lotus Notes and Oracle Secure SQL. It is also used for secure communications such as the encryption of traffic to and from secure Web sites using the SSL protocol.

PKCS #7. Public Key Cryptography Standard #7 is one of a series of RSA Data Security, Inc. documents that describes an industry standard interface to public-key cryptography. It defines a general syntax for information that can be encrypted or signed, such as digital signatures and envelopes.

PKCS #10. Public Key Cryptography Standard #10 defines a standard syntax for certification requests. A certification request is sent to a Certification Authority (CA), which signs the request and turns it into either an X.509 certificate or a PKCS #6 digital certificate. The request is signed by the originator and contains a distinguished name, a public key, and optional attributes.

SHA, SHA-1. Secure Hash Algorithm. The National Institute of Standards and Technology and the National Security Agency developed SHA for use with DSS. SHA-1 is a revision developed to address an unpublished flaw in SHA. It produces a 160-bit hash, or message digest, for a message less than 2^{64} bits in length.

This discussion is not intended to provide a comprehensive look at cryptography. For additional information, refer to the book *Applied Cryptography* by Bruce Schneier (Wiley, 1996).

Trust Requirements

Let's discuss how we can satisfy trust requirements. Many additional algorithms and techniques are applied in practice; however, these descriptions will provide an overview of the process. To the user, these processes should be embedded in applications so that their use is as simple as selecting an option from a pick list or menu. Note that whenever a private key is compromised, all messages associated with that key are suspect. Users should be warned to protect their keys from unintentional or inadvertent use, and particularly from theft. They should also understand that appropriate authorities need to be notified in the event that a key may have been compromised.

Authentication

A digital signature can authenticate that the entity who originates a message is who he or she purports to be. If the private key used to sign the message matches the public key associated with the originator, then the identity of the user is authenticated. The digital signature is usually generated by signing a digest of the message using the originator's private key and an asymmetric public key algorithm like RSA or IDEA. Figure 6.4 shows trust requirements processing with a digital signature.

Confidentiality

Encryption is the method used to protect the confidentiality of a message. In practice, the encryption of data is best performed by symmetric algorithms such as DES or IDEA. To share this information, however, the recipient needs to know the encryption key to decrypt it. The mechanism often used in practice is to generate a unique symmetric key, encrypt the message, encrypt the unique key with the public key of the recipient using a public-key algorithm like RSA, combine these two components in a message, and then send them to the recipient. Only the intended recipient will be able to decrypt the unique key, and then the message. Figure 6.5 summarizes this process.

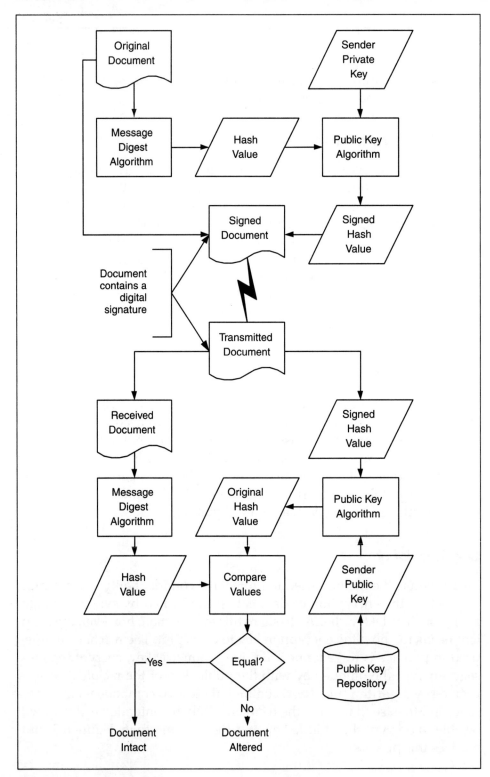

Figure 6.4 Digital signature.

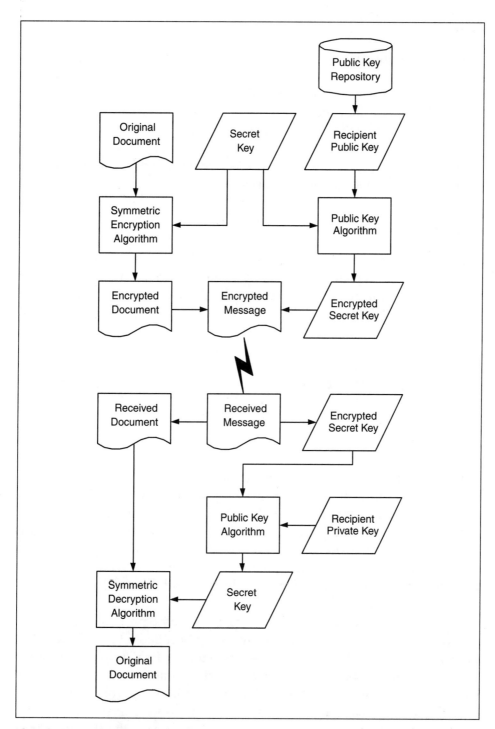

Figure 6.5 Encryption process.

Integrity

Validating the integrity of a message requires that a message digest was generated for the message prior to its transmission and that this digest is sent along with the message. One of the digest functions like SHA or MD5 is used. To ensure that the digest is not altered in transit, the originator signs it using a public-key algorithm such as RSA or IDEA using his or her private key and combines the encrypted digest with the message prior to transmission. These are then sent to the recipient. Figure 6.6 shows these points in the trust requirements processing.

Nonrepudiation

The protocol for nonrepudiation requires that the message be encrypted or have a digest created from it, be signed by the originator, and be time-stamped near the time of receipt by a third party that can validate the identity of the originator. Figure 6.7 shows time stamping in support of nonrepudiation.

Public Key Infrastructure

Public Key Infrastructure (PKI) is a business-oriented application of cryptography that allows an organization to satisfy the trust requirements we just discussed. Even though the previous section presented many technical solutions for the protection of information, the fact is that we need a scalable mechanism to deal with ever-growing numbers of correspondents. If an organization deals with a limited number of correspondents, the organization could conceivably exchange public keys manually. In fact, many organizations do this today as they communicate with those organizations with which they have relationships. In the Internet society, though, it is not always practical to exchange keys in advance, and so the need for a security mechanism like PKI arose.

A PKI provides a number of capabilities. Figure 6.8 provides a summary of PKI activities. A PKI is managed by an entity called a Certification Authority (CA). The CA, or a designee known as a Registration Authority (RA), physically associates and certifies that a name is tied to a person or legal entity, creating an identity. Second, the CA issues, revokes, and maintains digital certificates for an identity, and provides assurances that the identity is legitimate. Third, it develops relationships with other PKIs that

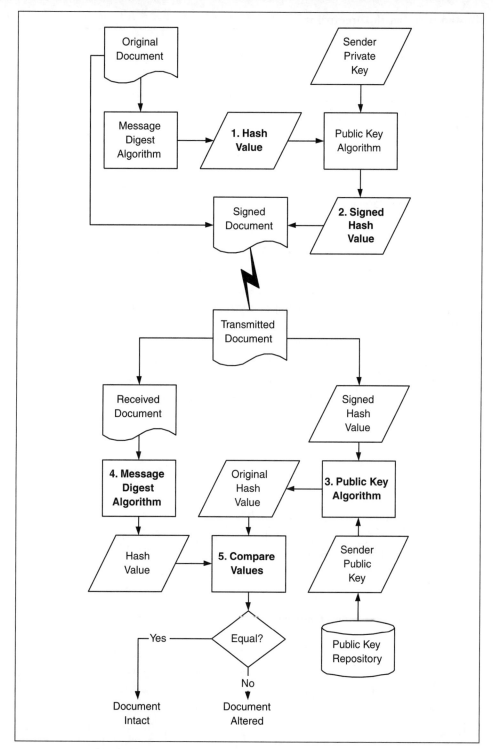

Figure 6.6 Generate hash, sign, decrypt, generate hash, compare.

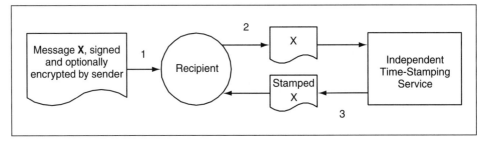

Figure 6.7 Time stamping.

enable digital certificates issued by one CA to be trusted by another CA. This hierarchy of trust enables the PKI to extend its reach between enterprises. To establish these relationships, a CA must publish and adhere to legally binding policies and procedures that govern the operation of the PKI.

The core components managed by a PKI are the public-key certificates, or digital certificates. A digital certificate binds a public key to an identity within the legal boundaries established in the CA's policies and procedures, also known as a Certificate Practice Statement (CPS). A correspon-

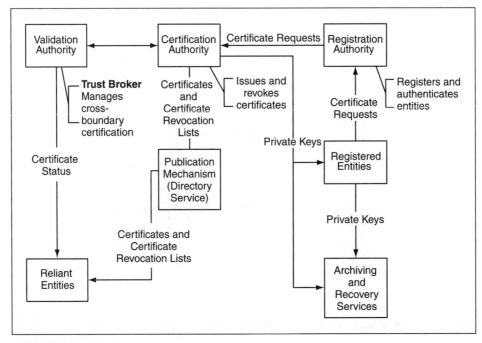

Figure 6.8 Public Key Infrastructure.

ding private key is mathematically and uniquely associated with each public key in a digital certificate. This correspondence enables a number of associated cryptographic techniques that rely on public accessibility to the public component of the key pair and the privacy of the private key.

Commercial providers like VeriSign and Thawte, which are certificate authorities, issue certificates for their subscribers and publish the certificates for access by correspondents on a global basis.

Directories fulfill a major requirement in a PKI by managing the information associated with public keys. When a digital certificate is created, the Certificate Authority places the certificate in a directory so that the certificate can be accessed by those needing to verify authenticity and to decrypt messages using the originator's public key.

The directory plays another role as well. Certificate Authorities must periodically publish information in the directory about certificates that are no longer valid. This notification is known as a Certificate Revocation List (CRL). Over time, a CRL may become quite large, requiring time to access the CRL and then to process the list to locate (or not locate, as the case may be) information about a particular certificate. The currency of a CRL is also an issue. Depending on the level of responsibility or value associated with a certificate, the CRL may typically be updated every one to four hours.

To address the issues of timeliness and size of the CRL, another protocol is in the process of development, called the On-line Certificate Status Protocol (OCSP). An OCSP server, called a responder, issues a signed notification regarding a certificate's status on request. The OCSP responder maintains information about individual certificates that the responder knows about. Maintaining a directory containing entries for particular certificates and their status so that the responder can answer status requests represents another potential role for the directory.

Other Security Applications for Directories

Directories play a key role in other security applications such as single sign-on, securing traffic on networks, access management, and electronic business. This section discusses each of these applications and the role of the directory in the application.

Single Sign-On

Single sign-on, also known as *enterprise access*, is the ability to sign on once and access multiple systems. Figure 6.9 provides an overview of single

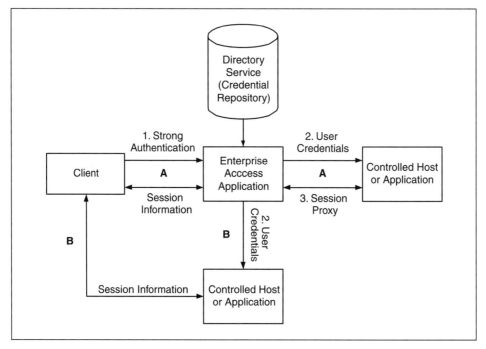

Figure 6.9   Single sign-on.

sign-on. Single sign-on is attractive to large organizations where users are likely to require access to several systems and networks, each having a separate login ID and password or other authentication mechanism. The more systems a user needs to access, the more likely that a security risk may exist. When users have multiple IDs and passwords to remember, users are likely to write the sign-ons down or use simple passwords that are easier to remember than safer, but more complicated, passwords. Both simple passwords and written passwords used as a memory support device represent risk to the security of an installation.

A number of applications in the marketplace attempt to address this risk. Directories play a role by maintaining a repository about a user and all of the systems and applications he or she can access. Combined with other network and application support activities, this represents the potential to consolidate a number of administrative activities into a single point of focus. For single sign-on products, the directory can act as a repository that supports authentication. Directories can also support the applications that act as proxies to represent users as they access the systems and applications they need. Even if an organization is not implementing single sign-on, the directory can act as a central repository for administrative functions like password management.

The debate over whether a single sign-on represents a risk greater than multiple sign-ons is ongoing. Some industry consultants predict that the implementation of "fewer sign-ons" is more desirable than a single sign-on solution.

Intranets, Extranets, Remote Access, and Virtual Private Networks

As we discussed earlier in this chapter, network access is accomplished using both simple and strong authentication techniques. The weakest authentication technique is the Password Authentication Protocol (PAP), which uses a combination of username and password to validate the identity of a user. A protocol that represents a stronger form of authentication is the Challenge-Handshake Authentication Protocol (CHAP). CHAP uses a username, password, and shared secret key to issue challenges periodically throughout a session to make sure that the client is who it says it is. Both PAP and CHAP are used by RADIUS, the Remote Access Dial In User Service. A directory can be used as a retrieval mechanism for key and access control information in these environments.

Virtual Private Network techniques use tunneling protocols that may encrypt the data passing through the tunnel. Microsoft's Point to Point Tunneling Protocol (PPTP), AltaVista's AltaVista Tunnel, and the IETF's Layer Two Tunneling Protocol (L2TP) all utilize digital keys to encrypt the information passing between the client and the server.

An even higher level of security is provided by the IPSec protocol. IPSec uses public-key certificates to establish identity and to encrypt the data passing through the network. IPSec provides various possibilities for encrypting the data, which are established when the security association is established. Distinct from IPSec, the Internet Security Association and Key Management Protocol (ISAKMP) is used to establish the sessions and the key exchanges. IPSec is the protocol chosen for passing information on industry extranets such as the Automotive Network Exchange (ANX). In all of these cases, the directory can serve as the repository for key-based security information.

An *intranet* is a private network that contains multiple shared resources available to subscribers to that network, usually employees. The intranet usually supports TCP/IP in addition to other networking protocols like IPX, SNA, NetBIOS, and others. TCP/IP is becoming the protocol of choice for shared resources within most organizations, as evidenced by its adoption by Microsoft, Novell, IBM, and others. The intranet may or may not be bounded by firewalls that provide access to and from the public Internet. Remote dial-in access may also be supported. In effect, the key characteristic of an intranet is that it serves a discrete set of users, typically the employees of one organization. The security boundaries of the intranet are very clearly defined.

An *extranet* represents the extension of the logical boundaries of an intranet to include customers, trading partners, and other correspondents. These users are generally provided access to the organization's intranet, similar to employees' access. Alternatively, organizations provide a shared network that contains segregated information and applications to meet the specific needs of the business relationship. In some cases, networks are interconnected between organizations to form an extranet. The use of firewalls to manage boundaries and access is almost universal, in addition to products from companies like DASCOM, enCommerce, Netegrity, and Securant that manage access to resources. Security concerns with extranets become very prominent as control over the community of users and the boundaries of the environment become more fluid.

A number of the protocols used to secure the network are candidates for the use of a centralized directory to manage user- or network-related information. Although they may not utilize an external directory today, the following descriptions provide an overview of how several of these protocols operate, including an emphasis on directory-enabled information management.

Remote Access

One of the services for remote access is known as Remote Authentication Dial In User Service (RADIUS). Figure 6.10 shows an overview of how RADIUS provides authenticated access to the network using a username and password. These are stored in a user profile database to which the RADIUS server has access. Each user entry identifies access conditions, such as the password, and may also include information such as the port or client that the client can use for access. RADIUS uses either the Password Authentication Protocol or Challenge-Handshake Authentication Protocol to validate user access.

Password Authentication Protocol (PAP)

The Password Authentication Protocol provides a rudimentary method for a client to establish its identity using a two-way handshake after the initial

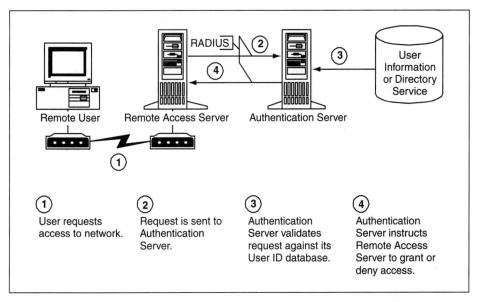

Figure 6.10   RADIUS.

link session has been established. The client provides an ID/password pair to the authenticator until the authentication is acknowledged or the connection is terminated. Once authentication is established, there are no further efforts to establish the identity of the client. PAP is relatively insecure in that the ID/password pair is passed in the clear on the network, and there is no protection against intrusion methods such as playback.

Challenge-Handshake Authentication Protocol (CHAP)

The Challenge-Handshake Authentication Protocol provides a mechanism to periodically verify the authenticity of a client using a three-way handshake. The three-way handshake occurs when the initial link is established, and it may be repeated at any time afterward.

The protocol operates in the following manner: After the link is established, the authentication source sends a "challenge" message to the client. The client responds with a value calculated using a one-way hash function, such as RSA's MD5. The authentication source checks the response against its own calculation of the expected hash value. If the values match, the authentication is acknowledged. If not, the authentication source should terminate the connection. This process can be repeated at any time by the authentication source, and the roles can be reversed, providing for mutual authentication.

The information exchanged in the challenge value is variable and the identifier changes incrementally, reducing the potential for playback and limiting exposure to a finite portion of a session. The authentication method depends on a shared secret, something known only to the client and the authentication source. The shared secret is never sent over the link. The same secret can be used for mutual authentication.

Because CHAP provides a higher level of assurance of authenticity, it is preferable to PAP. The RADIUS authentication mechanism uses either the ID/password combination from PAP or an ID/password/challenge response from CHAP to establish identity. The directory has the potential to be used as the repository for the ID, password, and the shared secret associated with a client.

Secure Sockets Layer/Transport Layer Security

Session security using Web browsers and the Hypertext Transfer Protocol (HTTP) over the Internet is most often accomplished using the Secure Sockets Layer Protocol (SSL), which was developed by Netscape. It is used in both Netscape and Microsoft browsers, and it is incorporated into most Web servers. SSL and the Internet standards-track Transport Layer Security (TLS, RFC-2246) protocol provide for privacy and data integrity between communicating applications. In addition to HTTP, SSL can also support applications like LDAP and IMAP (Internet Message Applications Protocol).

SSL fits between the applications and the Transmission Control Protocol (TCP) transport. It has two sublayers, the SSL Handshake layer and the SSL Record layer. SSL Handshake is responsible for setting up the encryption to be used during a session. SSL Record encrypts and decrypts information exchanged during the session using the encryption established by SSL Handshake.

The server and client authenticate to each other using each other's public-key certificates. They then exchange additional information that allows them to establish a secret key for the session. The process includes the following steps:

1. In the SSL Handshake layer, the server is authenticated using its public-key certificate. A directory server used to publish X.509 certificates and Certificate Revocation Lists may be queried to validate whether the certificate has been revoked.

2. Then the client is authenticated using its public-key certificate, as described previously. In both steps 1 and 2, the Internet domain name associated with the certificate is also checked against the canonical Domain name of the Internet address from which the certificate was received.

3. The next step is a mutual selection of the secret-key encryption method and the exchange of the secret keys for use by the SSL Record layer.

4. Activity then switches to the SSL Record layer, with the SSL Handshake layer suspended until an additional handshake is requested by either participant.

Transport Layer Security (TLS) is very similar to SSL. TLS consists of a Record Protocol and a Handshake Protocol. The TLS Record Protocol resides above a reliable transport protocol such as TCP, and it encapsulates higher-level protocols. The TLS Handshake protocol operates on top of the TLS Record Layer. The Record Protocol has two basic characteristics:

The connection ensures privacy using symmetric cryptography for data encryption. The encryption algorithms include the Data Encryption Standard (DES) or RC4. Unique encryption keys are generated for each session, and they are based on a secret established by another protocol (e.g., TLS Handshake Protocol). Encryption is optional in the Record Protocol.

The connection is reliable. Message integrity is ensured using secure hash functions such as SHA or MD5.

The TLS Handshake Protocol provides connection security with the following properties:

Peer identity can be authenticated using public-key cryptography. This authentication is optional, but it is generally executed for one of the session participants.

The shared secret is negotiated in a secure manner that prevents eavesdropping. A third party cannot intercept the shared secret and use it to violate security.

The negotiation is reliable and prevents modification of the negotiation correspondence without detection. The negotiation session is secure; a third party cannot intervene in the communications between client and server without being detected.

Both SSL and TLS provide security and authentication transparently, with application protocol independence. As you can see, both directory services and the Domain Name Service can play a significant role in the authentication process.

Secure Hypertext Transfer Protocol (S-HTTP)

S-HTTP provides a mechanism to establish a variety of secure symmetric communications services, such as cryptographic message formats using PKCS-7, Privacy Enhanced Messaging (PEM), and Pretty Good Privacy (PGP). S-HTTP does not require client public-key certificates. This feature of the protocol allows transactions to occur without requiring the client to have a signed certificate. The protocol can take advantage of a directory-based certificate infrastructure, but it does not require one. Instead, clients receive information to initiate a secure session using information provided in an HTML anchor. No security information is ever transmitted in the clear. S-HTTP is described in RFC-2660, released in August, 1999.

Other security capabilities are provided for HTTP through security services such as https and HTTP Digest. In a unique clash of names, https also stands for Secure Hypertext Transfer Protocol, a capability defined by Netscape. https represents a Web protocol built into Netscape's browser that uses Secure Sockets Layer (SSL). Be careful not to confuse S-HTTP and https.

HTTP Digest, described in RFC-2069, is an extension to HTTP that provides a more secure method of validating authentication credentials. Instead of exchanging a username and password in clear text, a checksum is created from the username, password, and other session parameters. This checksum is then passed to the server. The default algorithm for generating the checksum is MD-5, thus the name *digest*. HTTP Digest assumes a shared secret and never passes this information as clear text.

Kerberos

Password authorization schemes over the network are considered a weak form of identification. This is so because passwords can be compromised by monitoring network data, by the use of password-gathering applications planted on clients and servers, and by a number of other methods. An authentication method that is achieving prominence in the networking community is Kerberos. Kerberos was developed at the Massachusetts Institute of Technology (MIT) as part of Project Athena in the mid-1980s and has achieved recognition as an open standard in RFC-1510. Kerberos is one of a class of strong authentication methods that use cryptography so that an attacker cannot derive information from network traffic that would allow the attacker to impersonate someone else. Figure 6.11 provides an overview of Kerberos.

The point of authentication is to ensure the identity of the originator and the integrity of the data provided. In Kerberos, there are three entities that participate in the authentication process: a principal, a verifier, and an authenticator. The originator is known as the *principal.* The counterpart of the principal is the *verifier,* the entity that requires assurance of the principal's identity. The authenticator acts as a trusted third party between the principal and the verifier, validating the identity of the principal. The method used to authenticate the principal is via a shared secret key.

In order to participate, the principal and verifier are both registered with the authentication server and issued secret keys. These keys are unique and associated with the identity of the recipient. Once the information transfer is accomplished, the Kerberos authentication process consists of the following steps:

1. The client initiates a request to the authentication server requesting permission to access a server.

2. The authentication server provides credentials for the client. The credentials are encrypted using the client's secret key, and they consist of

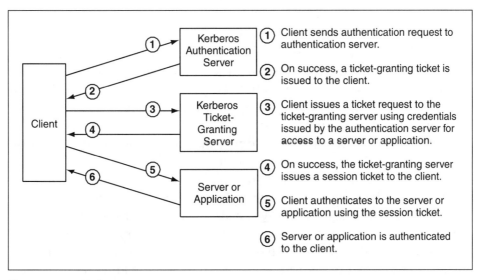

Figure 6.11   Kerberos.

a ticket to access the application server and a temporary encryption key. The temporary encryption key is also known as a session key.

3. The client transmits the ticket to the application server. The ticket contains the client's identity and the session key, and it is encrypted using the application server's secret key. The session key is used to authenticate the client, and optionally the server.

4. Once authentication is recognized, the session key can also be used as a key to encrypt information shared between the client and application server, or to exchange another key, a subsession key, that will be used to encrypt further communications.

Kerberos includes additional subprotocols that extend its scalability. There are two ways a client can request credentials. First, the client sends a cleartext request for a ticket to the desired server. The reply is encrypted using the client's secret key. This approach is used when requesting a ticket granting ticket (TGT), which can be used later with the ticket granting server (TGS). The TGT serves to limit the number of times sensitive identification information is passed between the client and authentication server to the initial request. Once a TGT is granted, it is valid for a given time period, say one day. The TGT can be used repeatedly during its validity period to request session tickets. The second method is where a client sends a request to the TGS. In this case, the client sends the TGT to the TGS as though it were contacting any other application server requiring Kerberos credentials. The reply is encrypted with the session key in the TGT.

Kerberos credentials can be used to verify the identity of principals in a transaction, ensure the integrity of information passed between them, and preserve the privacy of the information. To verify the identity of principals in a transaction, a client transmits the ticket to the server. To thwart replay attacks, the ticket contains information, known as the authenticator, that includes a time stamp. The time stamp indicates that the message was recently generated and is not a replay from an attacker. The authenticator is encrypted using the session key, proving the identity of the client because only the principal and the server know the session key.

To preserve the integrity of messages passed between principals, the session key is used to generate a checksum of the client message using a hash or digest function. The session key can also be used to ensure integrity and privacy by using it to encrypt the message. The directory can work in conjunction with a security service like Kerberos to provide identity information and act as a secure repository for the shared secret known to the principal and the authentication server. The directory alone, however, is not intended to act as an authentication service.

Kerberos is segregated into units known as realms. Kerberos is considered scalable in that it provides for cross-realm authentication. Kerberos is included in Microsoft Windows 2000 as well as a number of DCE implementations, and it promises to become a common method of strong authentication in the enterprise. As in the directory, the abstraction of security services like authentication from applications into standalone units will help to make these more standardized and universal, and simplify applications development when these capabilities are needed.

Tunneling Protocols

Tunneling protocols provide a way to encapsulate network data. One use for tunneling is to pass information embodied in one protocol across a network that uses another protocol. Some tunneling protocols protect the encapsulated information by encrypting it so that it cannot be examined in transit. In order to provide secure network communications within and between organizations over the Internet, several protocols have emerged that provide this capability. These are the Point-to-Point Tunneling Protocol (PPTP), Layer-2 Tunneling Protocol (L2TP), and IP Security (IPSec). Microsoft developed PPTP to enable NT and all Windows-based clients and servers to communicate securely. L2TP is a standards-based protocol that provides secure multiplatform communications. Both protocols are session based in that they are peer-to-peer. Another proprietary tunneling solution is the AltaVista Tunnel. IPSec is considered to be a more scalable solution than PPTP or L2TP, and it is being implemented on a broad level in organizations and communities of interest.

Point-to-Point Tunneling Protocol (PPTP)

The Point-to-Point Tunneling Protocol was developed by Microsoft for multiprotocol (IP, IPX/SPX, and NetBEUI) Virtual Private Networks (VPNs). PPTP enables secure remote access. It is available for the Microsoft Windows NT Workstation, Windows 95, and Windows 98 operating systems. Network hardware manufacturers have embedded support for PPTP in their products, and Microsoft has provided source code for developers on other platforms to enable the use of the protocol.

Users of PPTP use the Point-to-Point Protocol (PPP) to dial into an Internet Service Provider and use PPTP on the client to connect to a PPTP server on the destination network over the Internet. The server component is included with Windows NT 4.0 Server. The server acts as the authentication and access point to the destination network. Authentication protocols supported include PAP, CHAP, and MS-CHAP. MS-CHAP is a Microsoft variant of CHAP that supports MD4 hash as well as the DES scheme used in Microsoft LAN Manager. Encryption is enabled using RSA RC4. Many service providers support PPTP as a value-added capability. They enable PPTP at the dial-in access point, providing a low-cost, low-impact VPN service to their customers. They also support unregistered, privately administered IP addresses on the destination network, an important factor when considering the overall cost of implementing remote access.

Layer-2 Tunneling Protocol (L2TP)

The Layer 2 Tunnel Protocol is an emerging Internet Engineering Task Force (IETF) standard that combines the capabilities of two existing commercial tunneling protocols: Cisco's Layer 2 Forwarding (L2F) and Microsoft's Point-to-Point Tunneling Protocol. Like PPTP, L2TP is an extension to PPP, a basic component for establishing VPNs. L2TP supports multiple protocols and unregistered IP addresses. The protocol supports authentication methods such as PAP, CHAP, and MS-CHAP. The primary benefit of L2TP is that it takes the best features of two proprietary solutions and combines them to provide vendor interoperability in a standards-based solution.

Internet Protocol Security (IPSec)

IPSec is quickly becoming the protocol of choice for high-level network security on the Internet. It provides both authentication and session encryption and has been adopted for industry initiatives like the Automotive Network Exchange (ANX). IPSec can be employed to protect communications between communicating hosts, between security gateways, or between a security gateway and a host. IPSec makes use of public-key certificates to establish identity and to encrypt information. IPSec is intrinsic in IPv6 and has been retrofitted to IPv4.

IPSec consists of two complementary services:

Authentication Header (AH). The AH is used to provide connectionless integrity and data origin authentication for IP datagrams, and to provide protection against replays. In short, AH ensures the identity of the source of network information for as much of the IP header and upper level protocol data as possible. However, since some of these fields may change unpredictably in transit, AH is not a comprehensive service.

Encapsulating Security Payload (ESP). The ESP provides confidentiality for packet data. ESP focuses on the information being transferred, while AH protects header information. ESP, however, can protect header information if the session is conducted in tunnel mode, where the entire packet is encapsulated.

IPSec provides a number of options for information transfer and protection. These options are selected when a Security Association (SA) is established. An SA is a component of the Internet Security Association and Key Management Protocol (ISAKMP). ISAKMP is now known as IKE, or Internet Key Exchange. Key exchanges in IPSec can be accomplished manually or automatically, for example, from a directory service.

ISAKMP defines procedures and packet formats to establish, negotiate, modify, and delete SAs. IKE is distinct from IPSec, and it supports other security protocols like TLS. SAs contain the information needed to provide network security services like header authentication and payload encapsulation, services at the application or transport layer, or protection of negotiation traffic. IKE also identifies how to transfer key and authentication data without regard for how the keys are generated, the algorithm used, or the authentication mechanism. IKE provides a common framework for security association management, including format, negotiation, modification, and deletion of SAs, distinct from the details of key exchange. IKE provides a common set of services used by several protocols for establishing SAs, eliminating redundant functionality in each service.

E-Business

Governments, individuals, and organizations have come to rely on the Internet and other mechanisms to exchange trusted business information electronically. To support this growing reliance on the Internet, organizations need to do the following:

- Employ methods that ensure that the parties in an e-business transaction can identify each other
- Ensure that the correspondence between the parties is not altered during the exchange
- Determine that the correspondence is real and can't be disputed
- Prevent interception or misuse of the information during the course of the e-business transaction

These are all characteristics of trust, and trust plays a key role in both business-to-business and business-to-consumer e-business.

E-business, or electronic commerce, is not new. For years, companies have exchanged business correspondence electronically, using a process known as Electronic Data Interchange (EDI). Some EDI exchanges are conducted by physically exchanging magnetic tapes, but more commonly, businesses use value-added-networks (VAN) to conduct a transaction or pass information. In these cases, each of the correspondents establishes a relationship to conduct the transactions and formalize the relationship using a trading partner agreement or other documentation. The role of the VAN is that of a trusted third party, receiving the information from the sender and delivering it to the recipient. Some of the services that the VAN provides include format translation, time-stamping, audit logs, and acknowledgment generation. By using a VAN, a secure trail from originator to recipient exists, ensuring that the information is genuine. The major issue users of VANs identify is the cost imposed for handling each transaction.

The promise of the Internet and extranets is that the cost to transfer information will be very low in comparison to the cost of using a VAN. What organizations give up in this transition are the trusted third party and the notion of a secure communications link. In order to conduct transactions with a similar level of confidence, solutions based on the use of digital signatures and encryption have emerged to address the issues of identity, confidentiality, integrity, and nonrepudiation. These solutions utilize public- and private-key pairs managed in a PKI. As we have already discussed, the directory plays an important role in the PKI by serving as a repository for the public security information.

Summary

The potential role of the directory as a supporting mechanism for security capabilities is significant. The directory can be used to maintain security information about users, such as their login IDs and passwords to systems they need to access. It can also be used to maintain profile information such as access control lists for resources, such as a network, an application, or a file server. The directory plays a key role in the Public Key Infrastructure arena as the repository for information about digital certificates and certificate status. As the world moves toward a global economy using the Internet and extranets, the ability to access information that verifies that someone is who he or she purports to be, and that the information he or she provides can be trusted, will become more and more critical. Directories are well positioned to maintain information needed to support trust relationships in the expanding global economy.

CHAPTER

7

Network Management

This chapter discusses the role of directories and directory services in network management. Directories are used as network information repositories; directory services can be used to manage information about network resources. Directories are also beginning to play a key role in policy management and to support security in networked environments. This chapter also discusses several of the initiatives related to the role of directories in policy management, including the Distributed Management Task Force's Directory Enabled Networks (DEN), and the role of directories in ensuring Quality of Service on the network.

Introduction

Before we discuss the role of the directory in network management and some of the issues surrounding directories and network management, let's take a quick look at what network management is all about. Network management is the process by which resources attached to a network are identified and their performance is optimized as components in a network community. Network management includes the following:

- Using tools to identify network devices in an organization
- Developing profiles about network devices in some form of database
- Accumulating information from network devices
- Testing regularly that network devices are operating properly
- Analyzing information from the network to determine where problems exist and how improvements can be made in the network infrastructure

Network management includes activities such as inventory and configuration management, remote control, server management, network monitoring, print queue management, software distribution, application metering, application monitoring, virus protection, backup management, and data archiving.

Among the devices on the network that are typically managed are these:

- Hubs
- Routers
- Switches
- Gateways
- Firewalls
- Servers
    - Application
    - File
    - Remote access
    - Print queues
    - Proxy
- Clients
    - Desktops
    - Laptops
- Printers

Networks are becoming a universal mechanism for electronic communications within and between organizations. The boundaries and characteristics of intranets, extranets, and the Internet are becoming blurred as organizations seek to exchange information in real time. As these boundaries become less distinct, the need to control the performance of the network in order to ensure capacity and service is becoming more important. In addition, the need to control access to resources is also a critical issue. Organizations need a mechanism to control the devices and the mechanisms used to access and exchange information on the network, at the application, repository, device interface, and protocol levels. Network management tools assist in control, control of data, resources, access, and Classes of Service. The rest of this chapter discusses how directories contribute to the solution of these network management issues.

Directories and Network Management Initiatives

The promise of network management and directory services is more than just the identification of network components and their current state. Industry initiatives such as Diffserv (differentiated services) and COPS (Common Open Policy Service), and efforts by companies such as 3Com, Cabletron, Cisco, Extreme Networks, Fore Systems, Hewlett-Packard, IBM, Intel, Lucent Technologies, Newbridge, Nortel, and Xylan are concentrating on the potential for *policy-based network management.*

We have already defined objects as a collection of characteristics and information that model an entity participating in the network. Policies can be defined as objects, consisting of rules, that describe an overall business function and how the objectives of that function can be satisfied. Rules define a sequence of actions to be taken when a corresponding set of conditions is satisfied. Policy-based management is the use of policies, and their associated rules, and information about the components of the network and their current state to effect a change in the status of the network. For example, if the capacity of one gateway is completely utilized and others have available capacity, it would be possible to use policy-based data to dynamically adjust the traffic flow to utilize the other gateways.

The following sections describe some policy-based network management initiatives in greater detail.

Directory Enabled Networks (DEN)

Network information repositories today are generally proprietary components of the network management system. Directory Enabled Networks (DEN) is an emerging initiative, sponsored by the Distributed Management

Task Force (DMTF), to establish and utilize standards-based directory services to manage information about network resources. Initiatives are underway by a number of vendors such as Cisco, Nortel Networks, 3Com, and approximately 400 other participants to utilize the Netscape Directory, Novell Directory Services, Microsoft Active Directory, and other directories in this role. LDAP is the access mechanism for DEN-based information.

The DMTF set out to address network management issues by developing the Common Information Model (CIM) as a way to support the management of devices and applications in the enterprise. CIM presents a consistent view of the network environment distinct from the protocols and information formats they support. Although CIM is still evolving, it is becoming widely accepted by network infrastructure and services providers. CIM incorporates directory services as the repository for application and network devices. The Directory Enabled Networks initiative extends the CIM model by the addition of network-specific information that facilitates enterprise network management initiatives.

DEN Details

The Directory Enabled Networks (DEN) initiative was started as a joint effort by Microsoft and Cisco as an approach to use the directory as a repository for information about the components of a networked system. The intent of the initiative is to expose network services according to consistent and rational policies, and to provide the foundation for intelligent networks and network-enabled applications. Today, more than 400 vendors have announced support for the DEN initiative. As is the case with security applications, the role of the directory is passive in DEN. The directory enables network management systems to collect and maintain information about resources using a common repository crafted to suit this specific purpose.

DEN is not the first initiative to centrally manage network information. For example, the Spectrum product, originally from Cabletron and now offered by Spectrum Technologies, preceded the DEN initiative by several years and provides an enterprise view of multivendor network components, based on an SQL-based repository that acts as a device and policy repository. Other products, like CA-Unicenter and HP OpenView, provide similar functionality. DEN provides a shared, vendor-independent approach and extends these capabilities by using the directory as a universally accessible mechanism for network devices to publish and to retrieve configuration information. In addition, the directory is utilized to publish policy information.

Policy is represented by rules about how to configure and maintain network sessions based on the identity of the network user, the application or protocol in use, or some combination of these conditions. These network sessions must be configured and monitored dynamically, and they include all of the components between the end points participating in the session. Rules are established based on service-level agreements that the networking community establishes with its users. The logic associated with rules is processed in a condition-response manner, based on If (condition)–Then (response) constructs.

Figure 7.1 provides an example of the possible levels of service and how rules might be implemented. To help distinguish the levels of service, they might be named descriptively and classified as Gold, Silver, or Bronze. For example, a Gold level of service might be provided based on a combination of the source address of the request and the application in use. This could equate to a conferencing server establishing a data session between executive offices.

Representing policies that are more simple rules or combination of rules in an abstract and comprehensive framework will require significant effort on the part of designers and application developers. The challenge will also include development of rules parsers and policy managers to execute this logic in a highly demanding and performance-oriented environment. Applications will also be required to model and capture this rules logic in a simple and effective manner, and they will be capable of detecting conflicting rules in the knowledge base.

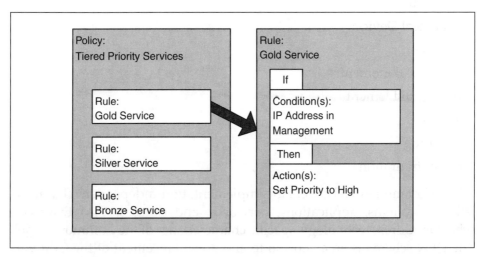

Figure 7.1 Levels of service.

The DEN specification identifies two types of information about network devices. The first is the dynamic state, or the information that is exchanged by network management protocols such as the Simple Network Management Protocol (SNMP), the OSI Common Management Information Protocol (CMIP), and the Remote Network Monitoring (RMON) specification. These protocols communicate with network devices. The second kind of information is the persistent, or static, state. Persistent state information represents information about network objects, such as their name and configuration. DEN is intended to provide a repository for persistent state information, and also to provide a mechanism to describe the relationships between networked objects. One of the benefits of having this information available in a directory is that it can be accessed centrally, rather than requiring an application to discover and contact each device separately.

The Distributed Management Task Force has an ongoing effort to develop a framework for the description of the characteristics of networked computer systems. This framework is known as the Common Information Model, or CIM. One of the goals of the CIM effort is to enable the enterprise management of devices and applications. CIM has been acknowledged by a large community of network infrastructure and management software developers.

CIM and DEN share many of the same information needs. The CIM schema includes a Core and Common model and an Extension schema. The Core model covers the characteristics applicable to all management areas, and it includes base classes such as these:

- Product
- Logical Device
- System
- Physical Element
- Logical Element
- Service
- Setting
- Configuration

The Common model covers the implementation-independent characteristics of systems, applications, networks, and devices. CIM Extension schemas address technology-specific characteristics of the Common model. The DEN schema is an extension to and an enhancement of the CIM version 2.0 information model.

The DEN schema addresses the identification and management of network device information in corporate and commercial network environments. DEN includes the following 10 object classes:

- Person
- Device
- Application
- Protocol
- Media
- Service
- Profile
- Policy
- Location
- Linked Container

The DEN schema consists of information derived from both X.500 and CIM, and it includes six abstractions of major network objects that extend the characteristics of the CIM model:

- Network Device
- Network Protocol
- Network Media
- Profile
- Policy
- Network Service

DEN will enhance the use of CIM by adding network device and policy information to a core information model about management, device, and system data, and by storing this information in a directory. Application developers benefit from the availability of a centralized repository that represents information in a standardized format. The user environment benefits by enabling the allocation of capabilities as required on a user or application basis. The CIM and DEN schemas are works in process; visit the DMTF Web site at www.dmft.org for more information.

DEN acts as the intermediary between the information accessible using network management protocols and the objectives of the CIM initiative, enterprise management. In addition to the dynamic information provided by protocols like SNMP, DEN is also capable of integrating other sources of information, such as that provided by the Management Information

Base (MIB), and standard network information applications such as DNS, DHCP, and RADIUS. DEN makes this information available using the LDAP version 3 protocol, which simplifies the work of product vendors by eliminating the need for them to incorporate yet another protocol interface like LDAP into their devices. DEN also addresses how to extend policy management, such as access privileges, into these environments.

DEN will be supported by multiple directory vendors, including Microsoft, with Active Directory, the Netscape Directory Server, and Novell Directory Services. By itself, the directory will provide a publishing mechanism. In order to realize the promise of enterprise management, DEN will require the development of standards for representing and actually implementing the rules or policies that enable Quality or Classes of Service. This work is being addressed in venues such as the IETF's Policy Management Work Group. Ultimately, common Application Program Interfaces and Software Development Kits will be provided.

DEN recognizes one condition that will also need to be incorporated into vendor strategies. The directory is not the repository best suited for the collection and provision of transactional and volatile data like state information. Vendors will need to address how best to integrate the directory as the common repository with other stores identifying the dynamic conditions present on the network. These special-purpose stores will contain data such as the community of components that make up the specific communications path between components, and the manner in which policies are implemented in unique, multivendor environments that exist only at the time the session is established. It is highly likely that special repositories, such as file systems, databases, or memory caches, will be implemented by vendors to track these conditions. The directory, however, will still play a role in identifying the location and characteristics of these repositories.

At the time of this writing, the DEN specification was still in the approval process. Many of the core schema components have been incorporated by vendors into their directory and networking products, if only to leverage common understanding and to hasten development. The DEN specifications have been incorporated into the Common Information Model (CIM) by the DMTF. The real impact of DEN will begin to be felt over the next several years as implementers begin to understand DEN's capabilities and incorporate them into DEN-enabled products.

Policy Management

The Policy Framework Working Group of the IETF is developing a secure framework for policy administration. They are also developing a model for the representation and distribution of multiple devices and device types. These devices include those whose primary role is to enforce a policy as well as devices that have one or more of the following roles: policy storage, distribution, decision making, conflict detection, conflict resolution, administration, and management. Figure 7.2 shows the essential elements of the IETF model.

The need to provide a predictable way of allocating network resources based on application, user, or protocol priority is significant in the era of the intelligent network. Just having a repository of information about the components and users of a network accomplishes little; a means to effectively utilize this information in a standard and consistent manner is the driving

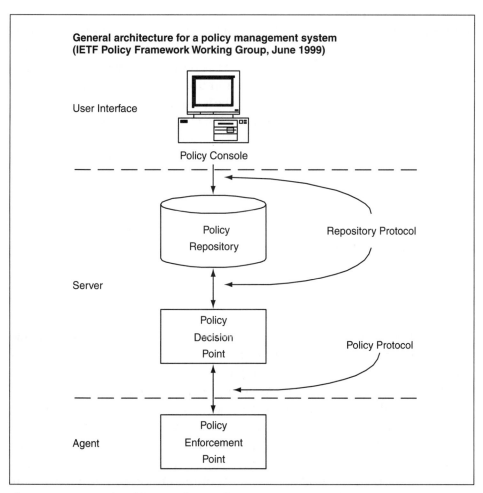

Figure 7.2 General architecture for a policy management system.

force behind the efforts of the Policy Framework Working Group. Some of the standard protocols under development include the Common Open Policy Service (COPS), Resource Reservation Setup Protocol (RSVP), and others. These standard protocols enable the application of established policy rules in order to ensure a consistent and repeatable level of service based on specific conditions. The use of policies helps reduce the cost of network resources by promoting their effective utilization. In addition, management costs associated with the network are reduced by the implementation of an automated framework that manages services such as traffic prioritization, traffic management, event correlation, event filtering, and the realization of service-level agreements.

When more network management functions are automated, doing so eliminates the need for manual intervention by network administrators. As a result, organizations benefit from lower infrastructure investments and reduced administration costs. Organizations reap benefits from the ability to effectively tie technical capabilities such as service provisioning to business practices. Once the connection is made between service and business, results such as leveling out traffic flow and the ability to give priority to users and applications during peak periods can be realized.

The goal of the Policy Framework Working Group is to develop a vendor- and device-independent specification identifying what a device or resource must do to provide the desired services. This approach will promote interoperability across multiple platforms. By developing a common schema and practice for managing network information, the DMTF's development of the Common Information Model (CIM) and the DEN initiative provides the shared information structure. The Policy Framework Working Group is utilizing this structure to accomplish network management in a standardized way.

Considerations

DEN and policy management capabilities won't come without investments in new infrastructure. Organizations and service providers will need to incorporate DEN-capable network hardware, management tools, and the associated directory services in order to realize these benefits.

A centralized directory service is also needed to tie together the disparate network resource information, provide a central point of access and administration for resource information, and represent the associated policy framework. The directory must provide high performance on a continuous basis in order to accommodate the needs of the underlying infrastructure, to address level-of-service expectations as high as or higher than the network. Achieving these levels of performance will require investment in tested platforms that provide interoperability with network hardware, using scalable and robust solutions with capabilities such as fail-over and fault tolerance. These platforms are not inexpensive, and they must be simple to operate, manage, and maintain. The directory service may also need to be dedicated, operating with physical independence from others in the organization, even if it shares a logical branch in the directory hierarchy, and participates by sharing some of the information from other corporate directories. Meta-directory technology may be employed to provide the population and exchange of resource and policy information to the network directory.

More basic than the need for a capable infrastructure is an understanding of the benefits of an intelligent network and how it will contribute to the realization of business objectives. Organizations must articulate their expectations for the extended enterprise and determine what role the network infrastructure will play. Service-level agreements must be developed that support the investment in infrastructure and tie back to business objectives. An architecture must be developed that expresses the structure of the extended enterprise, including those components that are not under the control of the immediate organization, in other words, that may be part of their partners' or service providers' network infrastructure. The capabilities or lack of capabilities in these environments must be understood in order to set expectations as to what may or may not be achievable by making the investment. It is becoming clear that throwing additional network capacity at a performance problem may not resolve the problem due to factors outside the control of the organization. The investment in policy management-compatible infrastructure may represent a more viable, technical, and cost-effective approach to the issue. The investment in a network management framework that provides the organization with visibility as to how the network infrastructure contributes to its business objectives is a critical component in the overall architecture.

The role of the directory in network management is just another example of how the directory is becoming accepted as the centralized repository for a number of interesting objects. In Chapter 6, "Security," we discussed how the directory contributes to the management of security. As we mentioned, the directory can play a role as a secure repository for information about network users and resources. The directory is equally well suited to maintain and publish information about policy, resources, and identities, and it can accomplish this role using well-understood interfaces like LDAP that simplify the task of the applications or device developer as well as assist users of the information. While the main focus of this chapter is how the directory can facilitate network management, the reader is encouraged to consider that the information that is utilized in this domain is also common to other management environments, such as systems and applications. The characteristics of integrated management capabilities and the need for a shared repository make the directory and management tools associated with systems, applications, and networks a synergistic combination.

Directories and Quality of Service

The term *Quality of Service* (QoS) has several meanings. Quality of Service is the perception of the reliable delivery of information, often at a level that is better than anticipated. The concept incorporates characteristics such as minimum delays, data integrity, no data loss, and the use of the shortest path between the source and destination. Quality of Service carries the connotation that these characteristics are implicit in the network environment. Quality of Service also incorporates guaranteed services that can be ensured contractually with service-level agreements between a client and service provider.

The primary objective of policy-based management initiatives is to utilize network capabilities to their best advantage. Today, there is very little dynamic capability in the network environment to react to the need for better utilization of network capacity. This means that in order to provide appropriate capacity when conditions warrant, networks must be constructed to address the maximum anticipated demand. This is like building a 12-lane highway in anticipation of rush hour when the average traffic between two points may only require 2 to 4 lanes.

Two models can be used to discuss network service: *undifferentiated* and *differentiated.* Let's consider two examples. Given a four- or six-lane highway, everyone on the highway has the same potential for reaching their destination by having to negotiate the same barriers and restrictions. The undifferentiated model makes no distinction in the traffic on the highway—everyone is subjected to the same conditions.

The undifferentiated model doesn't take into account special cases like emergency vehicles and vehicles travelling with two or more passengers. The differentiated model, however, does recognize these and results in a highway with special regulations for emergency vehicles and high-occupancy vehicle lanes for commuters. This allows the prioritized traffic to move around obstacles quickly and to have a relatively barrier-free passage to their destination. So it is with the differentiated model for network management. Traffic with higher priority is given access to more capacity than traffic with lower priority. The differentiated model represents a further refinement of the Quality of Service concept. Differentiation implies Classes of Service (CoS) in addition to Quality of Service.

With this distinction in mind, it is the intent of the network community to be able to identify different levels of service based on some form of standard or agreement. It is reasonable to assume that a service provider could offer three levels of business service, Premium, Standard, and Economy, each based on a different price model and service-level agreement. Personal users could also be offered commodity or class-less service.

Classes of Service for network traffic can be established by considering the following:

- Protocol in use, for example, TCP, UDP, or IPX
- Source or destination protocol port, which identifies the application, such as FTP or Telnet
- Protocol-specific source or destination host address
- Source device interface, which identifies how the traffic entered the device
- Flow, which is a combination of the source and destination host addresses
- Source and destination ports

Establishing a classification is accomplished by actively identifying the pertinent parameters and associating them with a policy or agreement. Certain protocols may also contribute to classification, such as IP precedence parameters or Resource Reservation Setup Protocol (RSVP) reservation requests. Based on the kinds of parameters and conditions that contribute to determining the appropriate level of service required, it becomes apparent that a repository that can identify the associated responses to conditions is required; this repository is most likely to be a directory in today's networked computing environment. Figure 7.3 identifies how an implementation of a directory fits into the overall policy management environment.

An in-depth review of quality of service can be found in *Quality of Service* by Paul Ferguson and Geoff Huston (Wiley, 1998).

Directories, Security, and the Network

A variety of security protocols is used to authenticate and access resources on the network. Today, few of these protocols utilize a centralized repository for access to their information. These protocols are seen as candidates

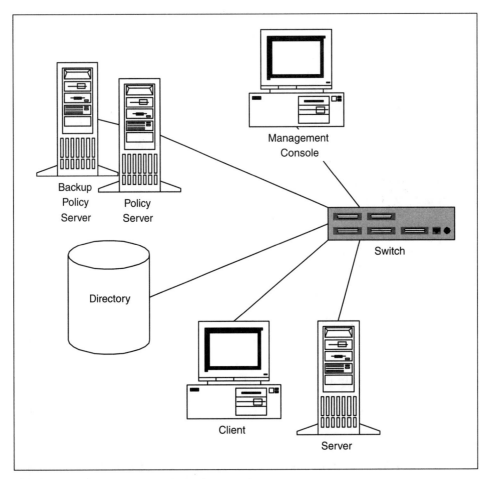

Figure 7.3   Policy management implementation.

for the use of a centralized directory to manage user- or network-related information. In Chapter 6, "Security," we provided details about their operation. They are identified here to show how they might participate in a directory-enabled information management environment.

RADIUS

RADIUS is the Remote Authentication Dial In User Service. RADIUS authenticates users to the network using a user profile database that contains information such as the user password and the port or client that the user is authorized to use. RADIUS uses either the Password Authentication Protocol (PAP) or Challenge-Handshake Authentication Protocol (CHAP) to validate user access. In these cases, the directory represents either an alternative source of authentication information using LDAP or an authoritative source for the management of access information that can be used to populate the database.

Secure Sockets Layer (SSL) and Transport Layer Security (TLS)

SSL and TLS provide session security for users of Web browsers and the Hypertext Transfer Protocol (HTTP). The protocols are comparable; SSL was developed by Netscape, and TLS is a standards-based effort based on the functionality of SSL. The protocols enable the server and client to authenticate to each other using each other's public-key certificates. The directory is used as a repository for X.509 digital certificates and represents the source for public keys in these environments using LDAP as the access protocol to the directory.

Secure Hypertext Transfer Protocol (S-HTTP)

S-HTTP is a mechanism used to establish secure symmetric communications services, such as cryptographic message formats using PKCS-7, Privacy Enhanced Messaging (PEM), and Pretty Good Privacy (PGP). S-HTTP is capable of taking advantage of a certificate infrastructure such as digital signatures residing in a directory.

Kerberos

Kerberos is a security mechanism used to provide strong user authentication using a shared secret. These keys are maintained on an authentication server and are associated with a user, or principal. The user also maintains a secure copy of the secret key. The directory offers the potential to act as a secure repository for these secret keys and for information about user access privileges in the Kerberos environment. Kerberos is provided as an authentication mechanism in the Distributed Computing Environment (DCE), and it is also incorporated into the Microsoft Windows 2000 Network Operating System.

Internet Protocol Security (IPSec)

IPSec is a widely accepted protocol used to protect correspondence between communicating hosts, between security gateways, or between a security gateway and a host. IPSec makes use of public-key certificates to establish identity and to encrypt information. Key exchanges in IPSec can be accomplished manually or automatically using a directory service.

Summary

Network management relies on the knowledge of a great deal of information about the components on a network. In addition to such traditional characteristics as location and configuration, network management is beginning to define and execute policy-based characteristics like priority of traffic and alternative routing. In addition, security requirements are also becoming more prominent, spawning key-based controls that rely on a variety of profile information. Bringing this discussion home, directories are beginning to play a major role in the exchange of identity, policy, and security information in the network environment. The most prominent initiative that utilizes the directory in this role is DEN, which is emerging in today's network products and management services. Network management services already on the market offer this capability; DEN provides a standards-based and vendor-independent mechanism to exchange information between services that utilize this information.

In addition to the management of network resources in the execution of policies, there are other areas where directory services may contribute to the publishing and maintenance of common information. This is readily apparent in the area of authentication, where digital certificates identify the user and public-private key pairs and secret keys are employed for encryption. The directory is already identified as the standard repository for digital certificates, and it can provide a secure repository for information such as Kerberos shared secrets and session keys. While they may not incorporate access to a shared directory today, many of today's network authentication protocols represent the promise of a centralized directory-based user, policy, or certificate repository. As organizations work to eliminate redundant information repositories, directory services will gain recognition as an enabler of these objectives.

Network Operating Systems

The leading network operating systems are Novell NetWare, Microsoft Windows NT Advanced Server, and Banyan VINES. Each of these has an embedded directory that is used to maintain authentication, access control, and other profile information for network users. Profiles are also maintained for shared network resources such as disks and printers. This book includes several discussions of these network operating systems in other contexts. Chapter 7, "Network Management," explores the nature of the directory services component of the operating system from the perspective that it serves as a component of an enterprise directory, and as the supporting directory for network-enabled applications.

Other popular network operating systems, like Lantastic and IBM LAN Server, are available in the marketplace. From a purist's perspective, Unix is also a network operating system, or at least a distributed operating system. Most of the underlying capabilities of today's network operating system (NOS) solutions have their roots in the mainframe and midrange operating systems. Our intent here is to address several of the most popular network operating systems and provide you with a basic understanding of the kinds of information maintained in the directory, the directory services approach of the vendor, and how that information can be managed and shared. We review the following for each of the major network operating systems in this chapter:

- Product overview
- Basic structure of the embedded directory
- Standards support
- Directory population and distribution
- Security considerations
- Interfaces to other directories
- Application Program Interfaces (API)
- Support for current or future standards
- Integration opportunities

The network operating system market is constantly changing. Fortunately, there is general agreement regarding the role of the directory within network operating systems. In fact, two manufacturers have challenged Microsoft by making their directory services available on Windows NT. The release of Windows 2000, however, will change the topology of the directory marketplace in new and exciting ways, at least to those of us who find these challenges interesting. To be fair, Novell has finally achieved the recognition it was due for Novell Directory Services, and Microsoft is playing catch up. Banyan set the stage early for NOS-based enterprise directories, a lead that both Novell and Microsoft are closing in on. The goal of all of the manufacturers is to provide a scalable, reliable, and ubiquitous service that applications and users can access for shared information about people and resources. The user community especially, and application development, are the beneficiaries of the competitive activity surrounding directories.

NetWare and NDS

In the releases of Novell NetWare prior to version 4.x, Novell maintained user and resource information in a repository known as the *Bindery*. The information in the Bindery was tied to a particular server, so that a user was required to log into individual servers to access resources.

This approach limited the scalability of the operating system. Even though the number of users supported by a server could be quite large, user access was oriented around departments and workgroups and made it impractical from a management perspective to support users desiring access to resources outside of a particular area. The Bindery was also mildly unstable and represented a single point of failure. Problems with the Bindery could render a server unusable, requiring the use of special utilities like *bindfix* to address inconsistencies in directory information.

Novell introduced NetWare Directory Services (NDS) as part of the release of NetWare 4.x. Now known as Novell Directory Services, NDS is loosely based on the hierarchical structure associated with X.500. Early releases of NDS were rigid in their application of the hierarchy. Once the hierarchy was established, it was difficult to change. The chief benefit of NDS is that the directory information is no longer tied to a particular server because the directory is distributed across all participating servers. One of the most significant benefits of this change is that the directory enables a single login to the network. Instead of being bound to a particular device, a user has access to the resources of the entire network, given the appropriate access rights.

Over time, Novell has improved the flexibility of the directory with respect to its structure and in the number of entries supported in a particular branch of the hierarchy. Today, NDS is available on multiple operating systems, reducing the perceived ties to a particular NOS environment and making it a candidate as an enterprise directory.

Basic Structure of the Embedded Directory

NDS is an object-based directory, with roots in the hierarchical structure of X.500. It supports the object and attribute approach of X.500. The directory in NDS is designed to manage network resources such as workstations, printer agents (queues), licenses, digital certificates, servers, users, and applications. Novell has integrated its management capabilities into the directory, including information distributed across the wide area network. It is possible to create local replicas of distributed information in order to improve performance. NDS for NT enables Windows NT application servers to be integrated into NDS so that NDS can handle authentication and manage trust relationships. The Groupwise e-mail and workflow suite can also be managed from within NDS.

Novell recommends that the structure of the tree (synonymous with the DIT) be divided into units, or partitions, each containing fewer than 1000 entries. Novell also recommends an organizational hierarchy, starting with an Organization, then workgroups, or Organizational Units. These represent container objects. Each container holds leaf objects, which are represented by a Common Name. Objects belong to object classes, which contain properties, or attributes, about that particular object type.

NDS ships with a basic schema, shown in Figure 8.1, that can be extended to meet the needs of a particular organization. The NDS basic schema has the following container objects:

- Root
- Country
- Locality
- Organization
- Organizational Unit

The NDS basic schema has the following leaf objects:

- Alias
- AppleTalk Filing Protocol (AFP) Server

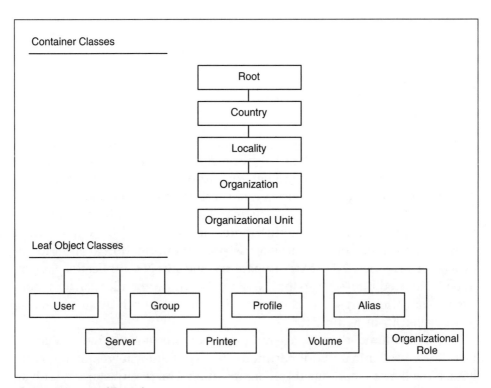

Figure 8.1 NDS hierarchy.

- Application
- Computer
- Directory Map
- Group
- License Certificate
- NetWare Server
- Organizational Role
- Print Server
- Printer
- Profile
- Template
- Unknown
- User
- Volume

Standards Support

NDS is a proprietary directory. It includes support for LDAP version 3 as well as the Novell Directory Services Application Program Interface. NDS incorporates support for the following:

- X.509 version 3 certificates
- PKCS#7
- PKCS#10
- DNS
- DDNS
- NIS

How the Directory Is Populated and Distributed

NDS is managed with the administration program *NWAdmin*. Information can also be entered into the directory from an import control and data file using the *UIMPORT* utility. NDS also provides support for the LDAP Data Interchange Format (LDIF). The directory is distributed across servers. Local copies of information on other servers can be copied to a catalog file.

Security Considerations

NDS includes support for X.509 version 3 digital certificates. Certificates can be used to sign and to encrypt/decrypt information. Servers and client browsers use certificates for authentication purposes.

Novell publishes access control information for file systems and other network resources in the directory. File rights include Supervisor, Read, Write, Create, Erase, Modify, File Scan, and (manage) Access Control. Management rights to container objects in the directory may be delegated to users by a supervisor. If a user has these permissions, he or she can create and manage objects in the container.

Interfaces to Other Directories

NDS provides backward compatibility with earlier versions of NetWare through a Bindery interface in the directory. LDAP functionality is provided to enable clients to read and write to those parts of the directory to which they are granted access.

Application Program Interfaces (API)

Novell provides the Directory Services Application Program Interface (DSAPI.NLM) for access to directory information.

Support for Current or Future Standards

NDS supports the following standards:

- LDAP version 3
- DNS
- DDNS
- DHCP
- NIS
- SLP (Service Locating Protocol)

Opportunities for Integration

NDS and NDS for NT provide a comprehensive mechanism for the integration of Novell and NT networks into a common management domain by developing a common namespace between environments. Novell's recent support for the Directory Enabled Networks (DEN) initiative provides a means to incorporate network devices into this environment. Support for DEN promises the ability to use Novell's strong policy management capabilities in support of quality of service and other rules-based management of network resources.

Windows NT and Windows 2000

At the time this book was written, the current Microsoft offering in the network operating system arena is Windows NT Advanced Server (NTAS, or just NT). Windows NT is a progression from the Microsoft and IBM OS/2 LAN Manager. Windows NT was introduced as version 3; Windows NT version 4 is the current version.

The directory included in existing Windows NT products is a rudimentary user and resource administration database. In terms of functionality, it is somewhere between the Novell NetWare 3.x Bindery and Novell's NDS. Windows NT Advanced Server attempted to move away from the limitations of a server-based directory by introducing the concept of domains. Domains are an arbitrary collection of users and resources, each of which uses a primary and zero or more backup domain controllers for distributed resource management. When a user accesses an NT network, the user logs into a domain, rather than into a server. Figure 8.2 shows the relationship between a variety of domain servers.

Within an enterprise, there can be one or more domains. Domains can be established to envelop users or resources. Users can access resources in other domains based on the establishment of permissions, or trust relationships, between domains. These relationships are maintained between the domain controllers for each domain. Using the domain approach, user and resource management in Windows NT can be centralized or distributed. For example, an organization could have one user, or accounts domain, and multiple resource domains, to which those accounts are granted access based on need. This represents a one-to-many approach and is practical for centrally managed enterprises. Several account and resource domains can exist, which trust each other in a many-to-many fashion. This approach works well for distributed organizations, but it increases the complexity of the management model because trust relationships must be explicitly arranged. Trusts can also be one- or bi-directional. The four domain models in Windows NT, ranging from centralized to distributed, are these:

- Single Domain
- Master Domain

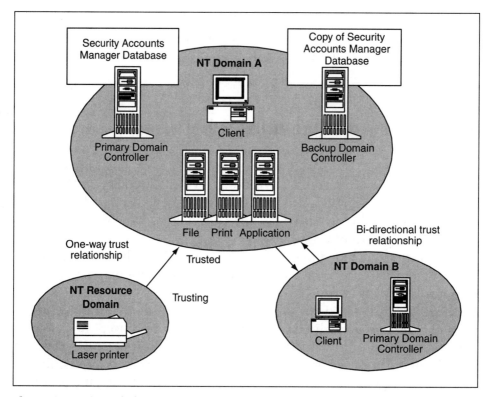

Figure 8.2   Microsoft domains.

- Multiple Master Domain
- Complete Trust Domain

Windows NT is a popular and widely implemented product, and it shares the bulk of the network operating system market with Novell. Once it is established, the Windows NT infrastructure works well. If an organization attempts to change the structure once it is in place, though, it may find that the Windows NT domain structure can be inflexible and problematic. Third-party solutions have recently appeared that help to address these restructuring issues.

With the release of Windows 2000, Microsoft will take great strides toward making the directory ubiquitous. The Windows 2000 directory service is known as Active Directory (AD). AD is based on the Internet Domain Name System (DNS) hierarchy for the distribution of information. The AD namespace is a hybrid between LDAP/X.500 and DNS. AD's namespace is a native LDAP directory that also incorporates a security management

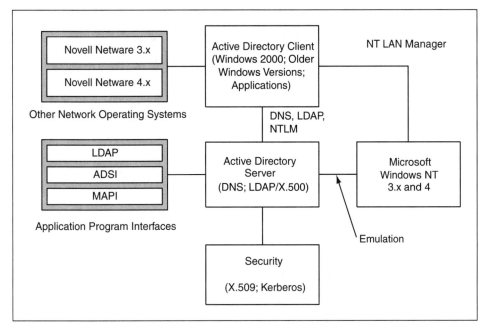

Figure 8.3   AD architecture.

model based on the Kerberos standard for strong authentication and authorization. AD will include support for Novell, Windows NT, and LAN Manager networks. Figure 8.3 shows the architecture used for AD.

Basic Structure of the Embedded Directory

The following section discusses the structure of the embedded directory for both Windows NT and Windows 2000.

Windows NT—Structure

The Windows NT directory is designed to manage users, groups, and resources within the Windows NT environment. Information in the directory is associated with security characteristics, and it is used to populate the NT Security Accounts Manager (SAM) database, which is distributed across Primary and Backup Domain Controllers. Each database entry is associated with a Security Identifier (SID). Profiles are maintained for users, groups, and resources. The characteristics of the information are identified in the following subsections.

Users

The information stored for users includes the following:

- Username
- Full name
- Description
- Password
- Confirm password
- User must change password at next logon
- User cannot change password
- Password never expires
- Account disabled
- Account locked out

Additional information can be associated with a user, including group membership, user profiles, logon restrictions to hours and workstations, account information, and dial-in access information. A user profile identifies the user's home directory (file system), profile path, and login script name. The profile path describes an area where the characteristics of the user's Windows NT environment are defined.

Groups

Groups can be local to a server or workstation or global within the domain. Privileges can be associated with the groups, which simplifies the tasks required of administrators. Groups that are predefined in Windows NT include the following:

- Account operators
- Administrators
- Backup operators
- Guests
- Print operators
- Replicator
- Server operators
- Users
- Domain admins

- Domain guests
- Domain users
- Creator owner
- Everyone
- Interactive
- Network

Resources

Resource permissions are associated with objects like file systems and printers, and they are managed using access control lists (ACL).

A richer set of descriptive and functional capabilities is provided for Windows NT by the Microsoft Exchange directory.

Windows 2000—Structure

The global namespace hierarchy in Active Directory starts with the DNS Domain Components, for example, DC=com; DC=tbg, and then assumes the hierarchy of LDAP/X.500, for example, OU=consulting and CN=Kevin Kampman. The DN would be DC=com;DC=tbg;OU=consulting;CN=Kevin Kampman. The benefit of using the DNS elements is that it roots the naming hierarchy in an internationally recognized namespace.

The Windows 2000 Active Directory uses the LDAP/X.500 object class and attribute model, including the characteristics of inheritance. In the releases of the software available at the time this book was written, Microsoft had defined over 1500 objects in the directory. These objects include those required for operating system and network management as well as those used to describe organizations, people, and resources. Windows 2000 supports a directory-enabled network much like that provided by NDS.

Standards Support

Both Windows NT and Windows 2000 provide support for a variety of standards. The incorporation of LDAP into the Microsoft NOS environment represents an acknowledgment of the importance of open access to directory information within information systems. It will benefit organizations by enabling the integration of diverse but related sets of information within the enterprise, and it will simplify the development of directory- and security-dependent applications.

Windows NT

Windows NT provides support for the following directory-related protocols:

- DHCP
- DNS
- WINS

In addition, Windows NT provides various interfaces to Novell's NetWare to enable client and resource access.

Windows 2000

In addition to the protocols identified previously, Windows 2000 provides support for the following directory related protocols:

- LDAP version 3
- DDNS
- Kerberos version 5 within Windows 2000

Interoperability with other environments has yet to be determined.

How the Directory Is Populated and Distributed

The Windows NT directory can be populated using the integrated administrative tools provided with the server operating system. In addition, NET commands can be used from the command interpreter in conjunction with batch and data files to accommodate large numbers of entries. Directory information is replicated between the Primary and Backup Domain Controllers.

The Windows 2000 directory can be populated using Windows 2000 administrative tools as well as the Active Directory Services Interface. The directory is replicated in whole or in part to all other domain controllers in the Windows 2000 domain. The notion of primary and backup domain controllers goes away in Windows 2000; there is load balancing across all servers so designated. Global catalog servers are also designated to maintain full global replicas. These provide information about resources within the enterprise that are not local to the domain.

Security Considerations

Windows 2000 provides a more logical trust model than the one defined for Windows NT. Implicit trust is granted within domain trees, that is, those trees sharing a common path to the root. Explicit trust can be granted to others in a domain forest, that is, those that do not reside on the same path to the root. Figure 8.4 shows the relationship between domain trees in the Windows 2000 trust model.

Windows 2000 provides support for the following:

- Kerberos version 5 strong authentication and authorization
- Secure Sockets Layer version 3
- Transport Layer Security using X.509 certificates
- Security groups

Exposure of the directory via LDAP will require careful design in order to protect sensitive information, either by access control lists or explicit restriction of information in the DIT.

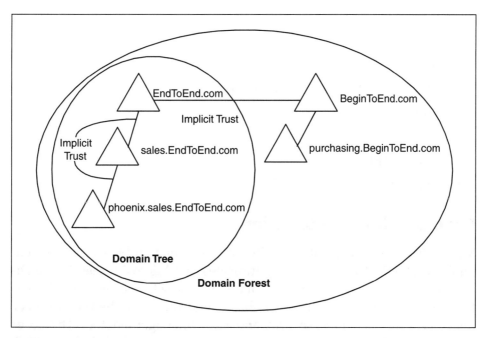

Figure 8.4 Domain forest.

Interfaces to Other Directories

Windows 2000 exposes its directory and interacts with other directories using LDAP. Microsoft has expressed reservations about LDAP replication due to certain security information in Active Directory not having a direct corollary in other environments that could inadvertently expose information. Instead, Microsoft submitted a draft document at the IETF for directory synchronization. Since this document was a draft submission, you should check www.ietf.org to review the document so that you understand the current status of the work on this topic. The recent acquisition of Zoomit by Microsoft may have some impact on Windows 2000 and its ability to work with other directories.

Application Program Interfaces (API)

Windows NT and Windows 2000 both provide APIs to their directories.

Windows NT

Access to directory information in Windows NT is provided using the WIN32 API.

Windows 2000

Windows 2000 provides support for these APIs:

- ADSI (Active Directory Services Interface)
- ADO
- OLE DB
- LDAP C API
- MAPI for backward compatibility

Opportunities for Integration

Microsoft's recent acquisition of Zoomit, a Canadian-based vendor that published the VIA meta-directory, indicates that Microsoft sees Active Directory as the integration point for many diverse sets of directory information across the enterprise. This is a sharp departure from the Windows NT directory, which is really a security and access management tool. The closer alignment of the directory with the operating system in Windows 2000, along with the significant acknowledgment of interoperability standards like LDAP and Directory Enabled Networks (DEN), is a clear step in the right direction toward a services-based infrastructure. Microsoft's reservations about open replication models indicates that there are still aspects of the information with close ties to the underling operating system that need to be managed internally and not exposed. Additional definition work by standards bodies may refine this next level of granularity to the point where truly open architectures can be accomplished.

Banyan VINES, StreetTalk, and StreetTalk for NT

The Banyan Virtual Networking System (VINES) is a network operating system long recognized for its ability to scale to large numbers of users and resources. VINES is service based, rather than server based, unlike Microsoft and early Novell network operating systems. VINES services include global naming and security across the entire network. VINES is built on top of the Unix operating system.

The VINES name service is called StreetTalk. VINES is usually employed in large enterprises, but it has lost favor over time to its competition. In an attempt to garner market share and to extend the capabilities of VINES to Microsoft NT, Banyan developed StreetTalk for NT, which extends the name service in a similar manner to Novell's NDS for NT. Although it is a technically competent and proven technology, the long-term future of VINES is uncertain.

Basic Structure of the Embedded Directory

The StreetTalk naming service has three levels of hierarchy, as shown in Figure 8.5. The lowest level of the hierarchy consists of items that belong to a group. Groups then belong to an organization. A VINES network can have more than one organization.

Items include such things as users and resources. A group usually corresponds to a department or workgroup. Groups are maintained on a particular server associated with that group, although a server is usually associated with multiple groups. For fault tolerance, group information can be replicated to several servers.

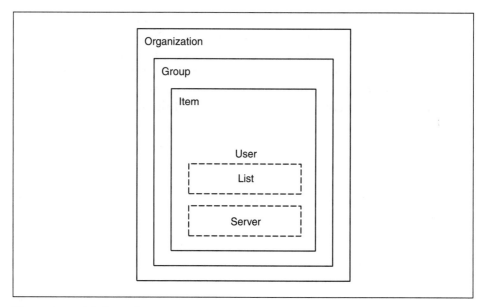

Figure 8.5 VINES naming group.

For small enterprises, one organization name is sufficient. In larger enterprises, more organization names are required. These organization names can be broken up functionally or geographically. As with all naming schemes, the approach should be well thought out and represent something meaningful and static in the enterprise.

Items, resources, and groups are synonymous with objects. VINES objects have attributes, or properties, that can be modified and extended. The classes that have modifiable attributes include Users, Services, Lists, and Groups.

VINES attributes are associated with the following characteristics:

- Attribute number
- Label
- Collection
- Value
- Filters
- Data type

An attribute number is a physical identifier for the attribute. It is constructed using a pair of numeric values in the form <v:a>. It serves much the same purpose as an object identifier in X.500. The v represents a predefined vendor or customer assignment; a represents an attribute number.

The label is the logical descriptor associated with the attribute, its name. A collection allows attributes representing characteristics that are closely associated to be grouped. An example would be Postal attributes, consisting of address, city, state, zip, country, and postal code. The attribute value is the actual data content of the attribute, such as "29 East Main Street" for street address.

Filters are used to associate attributes with one or more classes. For example, postal attributes are usually associated with Users, but not with Services. Filters allow attributes associated with a class to be presented when an object of that class is presented.

There are several attribute data types supported in VINES, including Boolean (logical), binary, string, integer, and ASN.1. Data types are used to identify and represent the actual data value of the attribute. ASN.1 data types are defined in X.500 and closely follow the binary data type. Attributes values are limited to a size of 4096 characters.

Standards Support

Banyan StreetTalk supports LDAP version 2. Support for LDAP version 2 is provided using the StreetTalk LDAP Service.

How the Directory Is Populated and Distributed

The StreetTalk directory is based on a shared information model because directory information is shared across all of the platforms in the VINES network. In a multiserver network, there is no single point of failure. The StreetTalk service maintains a database of directory information on every server on which it runs. Names are accessible throughout the entire network. Figure 8.6 shows how the shared information model might be implemented.

Databases contain information about each of the items in the groups associated with that server. In addition, a mapping table is maintained that identifies other servers and their associated groups. Detailed item information is maintained and kept up to date across all servers. Organizations exist as a logical mechanism to tie together or associate groups.

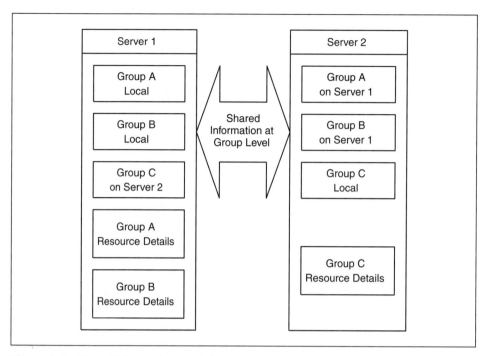

Figure 8.6 Shared information model.

Security Considerations

When exposing an LDAP interface through the StreetTalk LDAP service, care must be taken in the design to prevent inadvertent exposure of information in the directory, either by structuring information so that it is not visible or by applying access rights. The LDAP service exposes only read and compare operations to the StreetTalk directory.

Interfaces to Other Directories

The Banyan StreetTalk for NT component allows a Windows NT server and its services (for example, Microsoft SQL or SNA Server) to be integrated with the StreetTalk naming service. The StreetTalk LDAP Service enables LDAP clients to access information in the StreetTalk directory, and it also enables StreetTalk to execute referrals to other LDAP directories.

Application Program Interfaces (API)

Banyan provides the StreetTalk Directory Assistance (STDA) service, which exposes an API to application developers. The API is published in the VINES Application Toolkit.

Opportunities for Integration

StreetTalk for NT provides a mechanism to integrate a Windows NT environment into the StreetTalk Name service. This provides enterprises with a combination of VINES and NT to share a common namespace.

Multiple NOS Interoperability

In large enterprises, it is not uncommon to find an environment of multiple network operating systems. The bottom-up nature of most application deployments is also true of network operating systems, that is, they are deployed in response to a specific business requirement. In fact, it was more common in the past to see purely Novell environments than it is today. Applications are a major factor in the selection of operating systems, and the relative ease of developing for Windows NT, compared to Novell, has provided a major boost to NT's acceptance as an application server. This beachhead approach gave Microsoft the inroad it needed to convince organizations that it could manage the entire NOS environment, encroaching on the ground held by Banyan, Novell, and others.

Servers play many roles in the network infrastructure. Some of these roles include file sharing and printing management, application servers, proxy servers, firewalls, and traffic routing and management. One of the basic roles or services provided by the NOS is user authentication and authorization. The directory in the NOS is used to maintain these user profiles as well as information about network resources and devices. Some information about these resources is NOS-specific, and some information is generic. NOS-specific information includes data like the network address of a device, file location and access privileges, and the accounting information for chargebacks. More generic information includes ownership, location, capabilities and other profile data, canonical name, unique identification, login ID, and password.

The integration opportunity in a multi-NOS environment consists of the ability to share login and profile information so that resources can be managed from a central perspective, even if the tools are unique to their native environment. For example, a printer may be accessible from multiple environments, such as Unix and NT. Logical access to the printer is provided by printer queues within the respective NOS environments, while physical access may be provided via a terminal or print serving device on the network, or from a server to which the printer is attached. The ultimate objective is to maintain the generic information about the printer queues, the attaching devices, and the printer itself in a single location and distribute it to wherever it is needed. Sharing directory information between the respective NOS environments can help to meet this objective.

Extending NOS Directory Services

Products like Banyan's StreetTalk for NT and Novell Directory Service seek to abstract generic, non-NOS-specific information from the embedded NOS and integrate it into an enterprise directory that integrates all of the NOS environments. This "manage once, distribute everywhere" approach goes a long way toward reducing the cost of administration, improving the usability of network resources, and reducing errors and inaccuracy.

Both NDS and StreetTalk have the proven advantages of being able to operate on multiple platforms, scale across large enterprises, and describe information in generic and therefore more usable ways. Each product grew out of a successful NOS service, and each provides utility to other NOSs. Novell has been successful in extending NDS to conform to the DEN initiative, giving NDS the ability to manage network devices as well. What is compelling is that once this information resides under one roof, so to speak, it becomes much easier to leverage with directory-aware applications. Capabilities like single sign-on are now possible using a common repository, supported by profile and policy management that enables information representing business rules to be expressed without respect to a specific environment.

Microsoft's Active Directory will bridge the cross-platform gap in the Windows NT market, by integrating earlier Windows NT versions, as well as NDS, into its information environment.

Microsoft, Novell, and Banyan are all attempting to take control of the centralized NOS information management arena. The winner will be the provider that offers the most scalable, supportable, compelling, convenient, and economical way to manage NOS and network management directory information across the enterprise. It is too early to predict which solution will prevail, but the direction is certainly clear.

Summary

The directories associated with network operating systems are becoming service applications in their own right. Banyan and Novell have been able to distinguish the best capabilities of their directories and make them available in other environments. Novell has been most successful in this area, making NDS available for NT and several Unix environments. Microsoft is gaining ground by developing a product that provides standards-based access and the functionality desired for an enterprise NOS directory in its Active Directory. Although Novell is the clear leader in the cross platform arena, it is not clear that this will be enough to stand up to Microsoft's solution. Capabilities like profile and policy management and support for single sign-on will continue to raise the bar for these enterprise solutions.

Messaging and Collaboration

Messaging and collaboration represent two application domains that commonly include an embedded directory as part of the application. These are usually represented to the user as pick lists of individuals and groups. In both environments, basic user profiles such as membership, organizational background, and contact information are maintained. As secure messaging and security become more critical, digital certificate information may be maintained as well. This chapter provides a topical overview of the directory-enabled capabilities of a set of well-known products.

Messaging products in the context of this book include those used for interpersonal messaging, as well as application-to-application and application-to-user messaging. Messaging is considered one of the most popular applications in use today, and it is one of a number of capabilities known as collaboration. Collaboration also includes applications like group calendar/scheduling, electronic forms, document management and distribution, workflow and suspense tracking, and conferencing technologies (video, voice, and data). Other categories of applications, such as shared terminal displays in the X-Windows environment, also qualify as collaboration, but they are outside the scope of our investigation.

What Is Collaboration?

Essentially, collaboration is the sharing of information between individuals or a group. Usually, the purpose of collaborative computing is the gathering, organizing, and publishing of information representing proceedings or a consensus view of the group activity. Collaboration can be conducted in real time or at different times, in the same location or at different locations.

Lotus Notes is the seminal application that brought focus to collaboration in the personal computing environment. Notes is an application development and distribution environment that allows information to be collected and distributed among a community of users. Notes is usually associated with the term *groupware*; collaboration or collaborative computing is the expansion of that term to include the more global perspective on shared applications, such as conferencing and the others listed previously. Some of these applications, such as chat functions, are based on standards-based work, such as the Internet Relay Chat (IRC, RFC-1459) facility. Whiteboarding is defined in the ITU T.120 standard. Areas such as workflow are more proprietary—standards work has hardly begun for applications such as workflow.

Today, most collaborative applications are highly proprietary. Work is being done to identify standards, but in many cases, like calendar/scheduling, the nature of the beast makes standards development a difficult undertaking (read years), and solutions are only beginning to emerge. Work on the SMTP protocol began in the early 1980s; its emergence as the standard for electronic messaging may seem rapid compared to the glacial pace at which some collaboration standards will emerge.

What makes collaboration interesting from our perspective is the use of user lists and profiles to identify participants in the community of interest. Even at the dawning of applications like LAN-based electronic messaging, address lists were an integral component. Over time, the distribution and integration capabilities for address information became quite sophisticated, and barriers between systems were broken down using tools for directory synchronization and application integration.

The following discussions profile the directory components of a popular, but certainly not all-inclusive, set of messaging and collaborative applications. Even though the applications are organized into categories, making the distinction between a messaging or a collaborative environment is becoming difficult. The feature sets of the products are converging on a collaborative set of capabilities, of which messaging is only a part. Our intent in the chapter is to introduce you to the kinds of information each application maintains, the approach of the developer toward directory services, and how that information can be managed and shared. Our survey identifies the following:

- Basic product overview
- Basic structure of the embedded directory
- Standards support
- How the directory is populated and distributed within its application domain
- Underlying dependencies, such as to the operating system
- Security considerations
- Interfaces to other directories, such as an LDAP or X.500 directory
- Application Program Interfaces (API), if any, to the directory
- Opportunities for integration

The discussions are purposefully directed at a moving target. Ultimately, the applications should all share in a common and universal directory service. That's nirvana. In the interim, at least over the next three to five years, we can hope for shared information from multiple repositories that is consistent across the enterprise.

LAN-Based E-Mail

As one of the earliest forms of e-mail, LAN-based applications are widespread and take many forms. This section discusses many of the currently popular LAN-based e-mail applications.

Lotus Notes/Domino

Until the release of version 4.5, Lotus Notes was a tightly integrated application development environment built around a client/server database architecture. Notes provided standard capabilities like messaging and workflow, an integrated directory, document and image management, and threaded discussions. Notes also supported network-connected and remote users. As a messaging solution, what distinguished Notes from competitors like Microsoft and Novell was its platform independence. Notes is supported on Windows NT, IBM OS/2 Warp Server, IBM OS/390 and OS/400, various Unix platforms including IBM AIX, Sun Solaris, and HP-UX, and, until recently, on Novell.

Given the seminal influence of the World Wide Web, Lotus recognized that its client/server approach needed to include the ability to provide Web publishing and application support. In addition, the Web environment needs an open browser interface, requiring Lotus to distinguish the client from the server platform. This major shift in product architecture resulted in the repackaging of Lotus Notes.

The new server platform provides the core capabilities of the Notes server and in addition became an open Web server platform. The server was named Lotus Domino Server. The Lotus Notes client retained the Notes moniker, and it also incorporated support for the Web, in addition to its own Notes interface. This discussion covers the Lotus Domino Server.

We are interested in Domino primarily because of its directory services capabilities. Lotus Notes embraced an X.500-like directory hierarchy from its initial release, and it was one of the first environments to use digital certificates for authentication, authorization, signatures, and encryption. Lotus Notes incorporates its own key issuance and management capabilities for identifying users and protecting information. At the same time that Lotus shifted to the Web paradigm, it adopted support for an open directory standard, LDAP, and for digital certificates, using the X.509 standard.

Today, Lotus Domino Server has been reinvented to support industry standards while providing backward compatibility with its previous client and server versions, applications, and data. In environments where there is a need for the collaborative capabilities that Domino and Notes provide, it offers a compelling story. In addition, the Lotus Domino Server is offered in two versions.

The Domino Mail Server provides messaging, group calendaring and scheduling, document libraries, and discussion databases. The Domino Application Server provides support for collaborative intranet and Internet applications, in addition to messaging. The Domino Application Server includes the TeamRoom template to create applications for information sharing and collaboration, and Domino Enterprise Connection Services for access to backend data repositories. The Domino Designer and Application Studio provide integrated Web development tools that underscore the Lotus commitment to the Web paradigm.

Directory Structure

The Lotus Domino Directory, formerly known as the Public Address Book or Name and Address Book, is a database that resides on every Domino Server. It satisfies two purposes. First, it is a repository of information about users, servers, groups, and other objects, such as devices. Second, it is used to maintain administrative information about the Domino environment, such as replication, mail routing, and task scheduling. Each Domino Directory is associated with a Notes Domain, or logical partition of resources.

The directory is organized into documents, which contain detailed information about directory entries. Users are represented by *Person* documents; servers are represented by *Server* documents. Documents correspond to objects; the contents of the documents correspond to attributes. The Domino Directory is physically named NAMES.NSF. Lotus provides standard documents that can be customized to some extent. Restrictions are imposed to prevent the deletion or alteration of attributes that are used by the Domino system or custom applications that make use of the directory.

Other standard directory documents include the following:

Certificate. Describes a certifier ID, including public key information.

Configuration Settings. Used to configure mail, LDAP, and the NOTES.INI file.

Connection. Provides server and domain information for routing, replication, and news feeds.

Domain. Defines domains for mail routing.

External Domain Network Information. Lists names and addresses of servers in another domain.

Group. Lists users and servers for mail addressing, access control lists, and server access.

Holiday. Lists holidays that can be entered into calendars.

Location. Provides communication and other location-specific information.

Mail-in Database. Provides location and properties of a database that can receive mail.

Program. Provides schedule of server tasks and other programs to run, like the Unix chron file.

Resource. Shows an entity that can be reserved using scheduling tools.

User Setup Profile. Provides standard user configuration options.

The Domino Directory provides three major features. These include the directory catalog, directory assistance, and the LDAP service. The catalog is a consolidated view of information about users and groups from one or more Domino directories that is consolidated into a compact database. It can be used locally or by remote users to address mail to users throughout the enterprise. Directory assistance provides users with the ability to search through multiple Domino directories and LDAP directories by following hierarchical naming schemes. The LDAP service enables LDAP clients to search and to modify information in the Domino Directory.

Standards Support

The Domino Directory supports LDAP version 2 and 3 access. It also provides support for X.509 certificates. Domino supports S/MIME and Internet messaging protocols, including SMTP, IMAP, and POP3. Other supported standards include SASL, SSL v 3, IIOP, HTTP, and NNTP.

Directory Population and Distribution

Systems administrators create directory entries by completing a document for each entry using administrative tools such as the Register Person Dialog. The user registration process includes creating a Person document in the Domino Directory, a user ID that is certified using the appropriate certificates, and a mail file. Entries can also be created using the User Manager for Domains in Windows NT, from text files, or by migrating user information from the following platforms:

- Lotus cc:Mail
- Microsoft Exchange
- LDIF (from LDAP directories)
- Microsoft Mail
- Windows NT
- Novell GroupWise 4.1
- Novell GroupWise 5
- Netscape Messaging Server

Each Domino Server has a copy of the Domino Directory associated with the domain in which it resides. Changes to the Directory are replicated throughout the domain.

Underlying Dependencies

The Domino Directory is designed to provide support for earlier releases of Notes, in addition to supporting the LDAP protocol. Both Notes and X.509 certificates are supported.

Security Considerations

Because the Domino Directory is exposed to LDAP clients, administrators should carefully limit the modification capabilities provided to external users.

Interfaces to Other Directories

In addition to importing directory information from the application-specific directories listed previously, the Domino Directory is capable of interacting with any LDAP version 2- or 3-compliant directory.

Application Program Interfaces (API)

Lotus provides a Notes "C" API that is capable of accessing the Domino Directory. Developers can also use the LDAP C, Java, and JNDI libraries available on the Internet to access the Domino Directory.

Lotus also provides the Domino Mail API (MAPI). The MAPI service providers work with Microsoft Exchange, Outlook 97, and Office 97 on Windows NT, Windows 95, and Windows 98.

Opportunities for Integration

Lotus views the Domino Directory as a strategic enterprise repository. For example, Entrust has issued a version of its Public Key Infrastructure application to manage digital certificates using the Domino Directory. Prior to its acquisition by Microsoft, Zoomit had announced a meta-directory solution that would use the Domino Directory as the central store. This product will probably never reach the market, but these strategic alliances support the Lotus decision to exploit Domino's directory capabilities on their own merits. The cross-platform capabilities offer an alternative to an NT-only solution in mixed environments, and the standards-based interface and interoperability are attractive to applications developers.

Microsoft Exchange

Exchange is Microsoft's enterprise messaging and collaboration platform. Part of the Microsoft BackOffice product set, Exchange is the client/server replacement for the file-based Microsoft Mail application. Microsoft Exchange was introduced in 1993 as version 4.0. The current release as of this writing is version 5.5. The next release is code-named *Platinum* and will be released for Windows 2000.

Exchange is designed to operate solely with Microsoft Windows NT Server. It extends the Windows NT security-oriented directory to include many of the characteristics and features of an X.500 directory. Microsoft Exchange provides collaboration capabilities such as a calendar/scheduling system, electronic forms, and public folders. The server provides rules processing capabilities, such as generating an out-of-the-office notification and message filing. The entire Microsoft Collaboration Applications Platform consists of Windows NT Server, Microsoft Exchange Server, Microsoft Outlook 97 and higher, SQL Server, Internet Information Server, Internet Explorer, Active Server Pages, and Microsoft Visual InterDev. The typical messaging client used with Exchange is Microsoft Outlook, although any MAPI-compliant application can access Exchange. Web clients can also access Exchange when the Internet Information Server is installed and configured to support messaging access.

Directory Structure

The Exchange directory is a centralized repository of information about objects. It is based on standard X.500 objects, with additional Microsoft objects. Information that is stored in the directory includes the characteristics of the server organization, including addresses, mailboxes, distribution lists, and public folders, as well as configuration information about sites and servers. The Exchange directory is used to generate the Exchange Address Book, which contains information about users and can be used to address messages. The Address book is organized into lists, such as the global address list, and contains information about all of the users in an organization.

Standards Support

Exchange provides support for MAPI, IMAP4, POP3, and HTML clients. Within Exchange, standards such as Remote Procedure Calls (RPC), X.400, and X.500 are employed, as well as support for LDAP clients.

Exchange utilizes the following components, or connectors, to enable messaging interoperability with other systems:

- Internet Mail Service
- Microsoft Mail Connector
- X.400 Connector
- Microsoft Exchange Connector for Lotus Notes

- Microsoft Exchange Connector for SNADS
- Microsoft Exchange Connector for IBM OfficeVision/VM (PROFS)
- Microsoft Exchange Connector for Lotus cc:Mail

Directory Population and Distribution

The Exchange directory is populated by either the Exchange Administrator program (ADMIN.EXE) or using the Windows NT User Manager for Domains, after the Exchange application is installed and the MAILUMX.DLL module is added. Directory information can also be imported and exported in bulk from text files, Windows NT, and the Novell NetWare Account List.

Underlying Dependencies

Exchange is a Windows NT application, so its range is limited to the server platforms that support the Windows NT operating system (Intel, Alpha).

Security Considerations

Microsoft provides the ability to implement encryption and authorization in Exchange by implementing the Microsoft Key Management Server, which is compliant with the X.509 specification. Master copies of public and private key pairs are stored in the Key Management database, public keys are stored in the directory, and private keys are issued to Exchange clients. The Key Management system also publishes Certificate Revocation Lists in the directory.

LDAP access to the Exchange directory can also be configured. LDAP is integrated directly into the Exchange directory. Access to particular attributes can be configured for authenticated and anonymous client user access.

Interfaces to Other Directories

Microsoft Exchange comes with the following built-in directory interfaces:

Directory import and export utilities. Utilize ASCII text files to exchange information.

Directory Replication Agent. Provides intersite Exchange directory replication.

Directory Synchronization Agent. Provides synchronization with MS-Mail.

Source extractors. Enable address information and distribution lists, in addition to messaging content, to be pulled from existing mail systems during a migration. Extractors are provided for Microsoft Mail for PC Networks, v.3.x; Microsoft Mail for AppleTalk Networks, v.3.x; Lotus cc:Mail (DB v6); DEC All-in-1 v.2.3 and higher; IBM PROFS and Office Vision; Verimation MEMO MVS, v.3.2.1 and higher; Novell Group-Wise; Collabra Share.

Application Program Interfaces

The Messaging Application Program Interface (MAPI) provides access to the Exchange directory.

Opportunities for Integration

Due to the huge success of Exchange in the Windows NT marketplace, it has become a focal point for both internal Microsoft applications and third-party applications. Straightforward access to the Exchange directory service by applications and its richer information content as compared to Windows NT make it the likely point of integration for Windows NT-based applications in an enterprise. The release of a fully functional directory and security service in Active Directory will help to extend the centralized focus that the Exchange directory provides.

Novell GroupWise

GroupWise is Novell's collaboration solution. It requires access to NDS, but it operates across multiple operating system environments. It provides messaging services, a personal and group calendar, task management, workflow, document and image management, telephony, shared folders, and threaded conversations. GroupWise employs the concept of a Universal Mailbox to represent multiple object types, such as tasks, e-mail, facsimiles, and documents, in a single view. GroupWise also provides server-executed, rules-based message management. The current release at the time this book was written is 5.5.

Directory Structure

GroupWise utilizes Novell Directory Services (NDS) as its master directory. NDS is used as a repository for information about Groupwise domains, post offices, libraries, gateways, users, and resources.

Messaging and Collaboration   173

Standards Support

GroupWise provides support for IMAP4, POP3, HTML, and MAPI clients. GroupWise includes Java and HTML support for Web publishing of documents residing within the GroupWise library. GroupWise supports SNMP management of its servers and gateways through its GroupWise Monitor snap-in for Novell's ManageWise system management environment.

Novell GroupWise provides connection agents or gateways to the following external applications and systems:

- API
- IBM OfficeVision/VM
- SNADS Gateway to OV/400, OV/MVS, and Verimation Memo
- X.400
- Internet (SMTP/MIME, POP3, IMAP4)
- HTTP/HTML Browsers
- Pagers

Directory Population and Distribution

GroupWise uses NDS as its directory repository. For this reason, at least one NetWare v 4.1 or higher server must be installed for GroupWise to utilize NDS for this purpose. The GroupWise Administrator is integrated into the Novell NetWare Administrator utility (NWAdmin). User accounts can be located in a single branch of the directory or distributed across multiple branches.

Underlying Dependencies

GroupWise Post Offices run on multiple platforms. Novell recommends that the Post Office Agent, the tool that processes messages within the Post Office, be matched to the operating system platform on which the Post Office resides. These platforms include the following:

- Novell NetWare
- Windows NT
- Unix (GroupWise 5.2 and below)

Security Considerations

All directory operations are conducted through NDS. Administrators require the ability to read and write to the directory, and to modify its structure when installing the GroupWise applications. Users require browse and read access to the directory.

NDS assigns rights to directory objects. Rights are given to a trustee (an object in the directory) for a target (another object in the directory). Trustees are given "authority" over targets. The Access Control List (ACL) is also known as the Object Trustees property. NDS objects have object rights and property (attribute) rights. Object rights include the following:

- Supervisor
- Browse
- Create
- Delete
- Rename

Property rights include the following:

- Supervisor
- Compare
- Read
- Write
- Add Self (to membership lists or ACLs)

Interfaces to Other Directories

NDS provides a service called LDAP Services for NDS. It provides read-write access to NDS based on permissions provided to the client application. LDAP services enable chaining and access to information residing in LDAP-enabled directories.

Directory synchronization capabilities are provided between each of the GroupWise gateways and the systems with which they interface, for example, OV/400. Specific capabilities vary by platform requirements. GroupWise also has ASCII text import and export utilities for the directory.

Application Program Interfaces

Novell provides an Address Book API for GroupWise, in addition to Administration, Object, and Token APIs.

Opportunities for Integration

Novell is promoting NDS as an enterprise directory. It is provided for multiple operating systems, is LDAP compliant, and has support from third parties like Entrust and Network Associates for digital certificate management. These certificates can be used within GroupWise for PGP and S/MIME signing and encryption. Although NDS is the oldest of the enterprise NOS directory services, it has received, perhaps unfairly, the least industry attention for its capabilities. Recent acknowledgments by Cisco for DEN and the porting of NDS to Unix and NT platforms make it a compelling solution, particularly in environments with a Novell heritage. Until Novell announced the Dir-XML initiative at the Catalyst '99 conference, no meta-directory solution utilized NDS as its directory. This will be Novell's next challenge, one that will make it a serious contender in the enterprise space.

Messaging Clients

A wide variety of messaging clients uses directories as part of their application. This section presents the most common messaging clients and describes how they rely on directories.

Lotus Notes

Lotus Notes is the client component of Lotus Domino and Notes Release 5 product offerings. As described in the section on Domino Server, Lotus made a strategic decision to incorporate industry standards and Web-enable its product offerings, and to distinguish the capabilities of the client and the server on their own merit. Notes is able to exploit the capabilities of the Domino Server and act as a Web browser, news reader, and messaging client, using one consistent user interface.

Directory Structure

The local user directory follows the same X.500-like structure used in the Domino Directory. A document paradigm is followed, allowing the storage of location, contact, and certificate information about Notes and non-Notes users. The local address book can access the Domino Directory over a network connection, as well as any LDAP directory. It can also use the distilled version of the Domino Directory, the directory catalog, to locate resources when not connected.

Standards Support

Lotus Notes provides support for the following protocols:

- HTTP
- SMTP
- POP3
- IMAP4
- NNTP
- LDAP version 3

Lotus Notes provides support for the following content standards:

- MIME
- S/MIME
- HTML
- Native image formats
- Java
- JavaScript
- X.509 certificates

Directory Population and Distribution

The Notes client address book can be populated manually by creating a new entry. Entries can also be added for individuals and groups by adding them from an open message or invitation.

Security Considerations

Notes provides a mechanism for signing and encrypting sent messages and for encrypting received mail. Either Notes or S/MIME encryption can be employed, based on the preference of the recipient. User certificates are collected and maintained in the User ID file.

Netscape Messenger

Netscape Communicator is a collaborative tool in its own right. Among its many features are a distinctive set of Internet standards-oriented capabilities including a Web browser (Netscape Navigator), conferencing tool

(Netscape Conference), discussion groups and news reader (Netscape Collabra), messaging client (Netscape Messenger), and Web page designer (Netscape Composer). The Netscape Messenger allows the user to retrieve mail from POP3 and IMAP4 mail servers.

Directory Structure

Netscape Messenger uses two types of directories. It has an internal Address Book where users can add their personal contact information and e-mail addresses. The Address Book also allows the user to specify LDAP servers that it can search.

The Address Book options include setting the search order of LDAP directories, how to display the results of a search, and adding or updating the list of directories to be accessed when looking up addresses.

Standards Support

Netscape Messenger supports POP3, IMAP4, MIME, S/MIME, HTTP, HTML, X.509 digital certificates, and LDAP.

Directory Population and Distribution

The Address Book can be populated manually, either by creating a card or profile for each entry or by selecting the addresses of entries to add from an e-mail message and providing an alias and other profile information.

Security Considerations

Netscape Messenger is capable of encrypting and decrypting S/MIME messages and authenticating senders. It provides mechanisms for obtaining a personal certificate from providers like Netscape or VeriSign and for protecting them with a password. It also allows the user to manage certificates obtained from correspondents who sign or send encrypted messages.

Microsoft Outlook

Outlook is Microsoft's approach to a universal collaboration client. It gives the user access to a variety of mail systems, including Microsoft Exchange, Microsoft Mail, Lotus Notes Mail, Lotus cc:Mail, and Internet Service Providers. It also supports Microsoft Fax and the Microsoft LDAP Directory. Outlook also functions as a personal information manager, including a contact information manager, to-do list, notepad, and calendar. The calendar provides support for group scheduling in Exchange.

Directory Structure

Outlook makes use of several directory services, including the Exchange Global Address List, the Personal Address Book, and the Outlook Address Book. The Exchange Global Address List is managed on the Exchange server to which the user connects, the Personal Address Book consists of names the user maintains locally, and the Outlook Address Book is the collection of names and addresses from the contact list. Outlook can also access LDAP directories if the Microsoft LDAP Directory is installed.

Standards Support

Microsoft Outlook supports the following standards: HTTP, HTML, LDAP, SMTP, POP3, MAPI, MIME, and X.509.

Directory Population and Distribution

Entries in the Personal Address Book can be created manually. They can also be created using addresses that appear in messages, as well as by adding the contents of vCards attached to messages. Addresses entered in the contact list are also accessible via the Outlook Address Book. Users can select the address book search order to verify addresses for names entered manually into a message.

Security Considerations

Outlook provides support for applying digital signatures to messages as well as encrypting the message content. A security page is provided to configure how security is applied to messages and message content, and also to obtain certificates from providers like VeriSign and to manage the user's X.509 digital certificates.

Novell GroupWise

The Novell GroupWise client provides the user with access to the integrated services provided by the GroupWise server. These services include messaging, personal and group calendar, document and image management, and workflow. The GroupWise client uses a universal in-box paradigm that presents a variety of different message types, such as e-mail, fax, and voice messages, in a single environment. Unlike Microsoft Outlook, the GroupWise client is tightly coupled to the server to provide a consistent perspective on information.

Directory Structure

The GroupWise client provides support for a Personal Address Book, in addition to access to the GroupWise directory on the server. The client is also capable of accessing external LDAP directories with the addition of an LDAP service provider, which must be acquired separately. The GroupWise directory cannot be modified by the user. The user can modify the structure of the Personal Address Book by adding or deleting fields.

Standards Support

The GroupWise client supports MAPI and LDAP. Support for other protocols is provided by the GroupWise server. Using a MAPI interface published by Novell, the GroupWise client is also able to access information on Microsoft Exchange servers.

Directory Population and Distribution

The Personal Address Book can be populated by adding new entries manually, by adding the contents of a vCard entry from a message, or by selecting an address from a message and adding it to the address book. Personal Address Books can be imported and exported, as can information from other sources. The Personal Address Book can also be shared between multiple users.

When a user is using the GroupWise client in a remote or offline configuration, it is possible to set predefined filters to limit the amount of directory information that is viewed or distributed to the remote computer. Users can select a feature called "Hit the Road" that downloads information that will be needed while the user is not connected to the server, such as address books, rules, documents, and messages.

Security Considerations

The ability to use digital signatures and encryption from the GroupWise client is provided with the separate Entrust Security Option.

Collaboration: Scheduling and Calendaring

Group scheduling is one of the more useful collaboration tools, especially in large organizations where getting people and resources together at the same time can be a Herculean task. On the other hand, the integration of multiple scheduling systems is one of the most problematic issues when migrating to a new solution, so much so that some organizations abandon the effort and just work with the new and old systems in parallel during the migration. Fortunately, group scheduling is primarily a workgroup type of activity, and migrations can be structured to ensure that participants move to the new system at the same time.

Group scheduling involves two primary activities: finding a time when everyone can meet and determining that necessary resources are available, and inviting or notifying the participants of the event. A third activity involves the participant accepting or rejecting the invitation. The directory plays a role in identifying participants and resources in an organization. Separate schedule repositories are usually maintained for each entity, in proximity to the messaging environment, which is used to pass invitations, notifications, and responses.

A number of solutions on the market accomplish these goals. The capability is embedded in Novell GroupWise, Lotus Notes, and Microsoft Outlook. Interoperability is an elusive goal; the most promising standards effort is the ongoing iCalendar activity in the IETF, which is intended to provide real-time and e-mail-based appointment scheduling. Group scheduling is usually available in host-based office automation applications like IBM's OfficeVision. Standalone cross-platform solutions exist as well, such as CorporateTime from Corporate Software and Technology and Meeting-Maker from ON Technology. Both solutions include interfaces to external directories. In the case of CorporateTime, it is provided with the Corporate-Connect product that provides X.500 and LDAP support; with Meet-ingMaker it is provided using the APS Engineering, Inc. Standalone Lightweight Access Protocol Daemon.

Collaboration: Workflow

Workflow is used to model business processes like the automated routing of forms using a database or messaging system. A number of workflow applications are on the market, in addition to a number of failed attempts. The trend today is for applications to utilize the underlying infrastructure of a messaging- or database-oriented collaboration solution, such as Microsoft Exchange or Lotus Domino, respectively. A successful standalone solution called First Class is provided by SoftArc, Inc.

Lotus Domino includes a separate product called the Domino Designer that facilitates the development of Domino-based applications. Workflow capabilities can be incorporated into these applications based on a variety of conditions. Role-based characteristics can be incorporated into the Domino directory so that routing conditions can be modeled by the application developer. Microsoft includes scripting and programming capabilities in the Exchange product as well, and several third-party developers have launched solutions based on Exchange.

The Compaq (formerly Digital Equipment Corporation) Workflow Expeditor is one example of an Exchange-based workflow solution. Another, the Work Manager Suite, is offered by Eastman Software and includes the WorkFolder Manager for Exchange. The WorkFolder is a collaborative container that holds documents and task assignments for users in a workgroup that are associated with a particular activity. The management software is used to track completion of tasks based on assignments and generate messages to participants based on events such as assignments and failure to complete tasks. The application suite makes use of Exchange forms and public folders, as well as the Outlook client. The Exchange directory is used to identify participants in a workgroup and to route messages. Status information is maintained in the folder itself.

Collaboration: Conferencing (Voice, Data, Video)

Conferencing tools are becoming an integral method for organizations to exchange information in same time/different location environments. Tools with varying capabilities are available to support the Windows environment, as well as Unix. The major players are represented in this space, including Lotus (Sametime), Microsoft (NetMeeting), Netscape (Conference), and Intel (ProShare). A developer in the United Kingdom, Data Connection Ltd., publishes a product called DC-Share for Unix that provides a Microsoft NetMeeting-compatible implementation of collaborative tools for the Unix environment. It is the foundation of products like Sun's SunForum, SGI's SGImeeting, and Hewlett-Packard's HP VISUALIZE CONFERENCE products. Conferencing tools include the ability to chat, share a whiteboard, share applications interactively, conduct file transfers, or view presentations using HTML as Web content.

Some of the standards used in the conferencing environment include the following:

- H.323 (audio and video conferencing)
- HTTP/HTML
- LDAP
- T.120 (multipoint communications over TCP/IP)
- T.126 (whiteboard)
- T.127 (multipoint file transfer)
- T.128 (application sharing)

As conferencing grows in importance, the ability to locate participants over the Internet or an internal network is important for peer-to-peer conferencing. For larger-scale conferences, the use of conferencing servers that support a number of users is necessary. In order to find these users or services, special locator services that provide a logical identifier and map them to an IP address are needed. The IP address associated with a user is dynamic when DHCP is used. Some examples include when a user dials into an ISP, or where proxy servers are employed. In either case, the user must register with a directory when he or she wants to participate in a conference, or else must provide an IP address to the participants manually. The preferred method is the former, which can be accomplished automatically by the client software. An example of commercial services that provide these kinds of locator services is four11.com, as well as ils.microsoft.com. The ILS provided by Microsoft uses the LDAP protocol.

Future Directions

The influence of the Lightweight Directory Access Protocol on embedded directories is changing the direction of the development community. Its influence is being manifested in several ways. Access mechanisms to external LDAP directories are provided in standards-based clients. Directory access for synchronization and management is being provided for central repositories. In the case of some applications, like Lotus Domino, the directory is being promoted as the central repository for the enterprise. For example, Lotus Notes has always had an embedded mechanism for proprietary user certificates. Domino is moving into the standards arena by supporting X.509 certificates as well as external certificate management software from Entrust. The Domino directory has been promoted as the repository for meta-directory applications, in response to the general industry recognition of the need for a centralized repository. Microsoft's Active Directory will also achieve prominence from this perspective, as will Novell's NDS.

What distinguishes Domino and NDS from the pack of Enterprise NOS directories is their application independence from the operating system. This advantage will become less distinct as versions of Active Directory, which are independent of the operating system, appear in the marketplace. The advantage that Microsoft will be able to exploit, however, is its recent acquisition of Zoomit, which provides meta-directory capabilities based on Active Directory as the repository. Novell is also moving into the directory integration space by adopting DirXML as the mechanism for exchanging directory structure and content information. This trend toward general-purpose meta-directory integration is only beginning.

Summary

Electronic messaging and collaborative applications represent environments where directory services were employed early and often as ways to facilitate interpersonal communications. From the user's perspective, the directories embedded in these applications are the most common personification of a directory service. Today, these application directories take one of two paths. The directories may evolve toward a common, shared directory such as that found in Novell Groupwise or NDS. Or, they may take the form of a more ubiquitous enterprise directory service such as that found with the Lotus Domino directory. In either scenario, these solutions incorporate LDAP as the *lingua franca* for accessing and maintaining directory information. The same trend can be seen in other areas, and the adoption of standards helps promote interoperability. It should be recognized that standards compliance alone does not necessarily achieve interoperability, since standards continue to evolve to address incompatibility issues. Organizations must monitor the maturity of standards as they design the architecture of their enterprise solutions and acknowledge weaknesses and works-in-progress as part of the overall terrain of the directory world.

CHAPTER

10

Telephony and Video Conferencing

Imagine that you could utilize a single connection to the Internet for electronic mail, faxes, telephone calls, video and data conferencing, and paging. Sounds like a recent ad on television, doesn't it? Well, in reality, these capabilities are driving the use of the Internet as more than just a browsing medium. Technology advances are increasing the likelihood that the Internet may displace conventional solutions, like the telephone. Corporations are eager to cash in on the possibility of using network infrastructure to avoid the high cost of long distance surcharges; they see the Internet as a mechanism to bypass long distance providers. At the same time, the deregulation of the telecommunications industry and increasing levels of competition among providers are fostering the creative use of network resources to offer services in more competitive ways. The proliferation of service providers in both the Internet and telecommunications arenas is forcing all vendors in the telecommunications industry to offer new and different services to differentiate themselves from their competitors and make themselves more attractive to their customers.

All of these efforts to use the Internet in new and different ways have far-reaching implications for directories and directory services, too. This chapter explores the role of directories in this fast-changing environment.

Introduction

One of the early capabilities that messaging community developers envisioned was the ability to bring voice and electronic messaging systems together. The concept of a universal inbox has made the integration of voice messaging systems with e-mail systems a viable solution. Voice messaging has been successfully integrated with Microsoft Exchange and Novell GroupWise. One of the leading voice mail vendors, Octel, was recently acquired by the telephony provider Lucent Technologies. This acquisition is another example of the importance of voice messaging technology in future solutions.

Providers of paging solutions, facsimile, and other technologies view the Internet as yet another transport mechanism to get information to the recipient, using translation technologies to eliminate the need for special equipment or services. A similar focus is coming to bear on other forms of communication. Conferencing technologies for the exchange of video and data are helping corporations reduce travel costs and lower the barriers associated with time, availability, and distance. Enabling the use of Internet communications in these technologies simplifies the connection process and the underlying infrastructure requirements needed to establish connections between correspondents.

As communications technologies use the Internet as the common connection point between multiple communications paradigms, as shown in Figure 10.1, the need for a common, integrated mechanism to locate entities on the network grows. The only scalable mechanism for this purpose is directory services. The need to locate entities extends beyond the boundaries of the organization to business partners and to service providers. The barrier to effectively locating entities is that partners and service providers each have unique mechanisms for mapping information about subscribers to services. The opportunities for directory integration in this environment are many and include the following:

- Mapping subscriber names to physical Internet Protocol (IP) addresses.
- Providing name lookups.
- Associating the universal inbox to the specific communications solution directory.
- Providing profile information about the user. The profile information might describe how messages should be presented; the presentation choices include image formats, document preferences, voice-to-text or text-to-voice conversion.

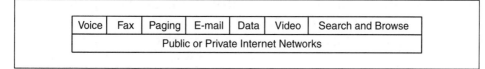

Figure 10.1 The Internet as an enterprise network.

Telecommunications providers and software developers must overcome many hurdles before technologies like IP Telephony become viable on a large scale over services like the Internet. For a comprehensive examination of the use of IP networks for transporting voice, conferencing, and multimedia related traffic, refer to *Delivering Voice over IP Networks* by Daniel Minoli and Emma Minoli (Wiley, 1998).

IP Telephony

IP Telephony, also known as Voice over IP (VoIP), relies on an organization's existing data network infrastructure to transmit digital conversions of audio inputs to a receiver capable of converting these digital signals back to their original audio form. Some early and current implementations of Voice over IP involved connecting a telephone to the computer. More recent implementations involve connecting entire Private Branch Exchange (PBX) networks to the data network using specialized voice conversion hardware that compresses the audio signal as it is translated to a digital carrier format. By masking the conversion functionality from the user, this approach is less intrusive and easier to implement from a management and deployment perspective. IP Telephony is very attractive to organizations that need to support remote or roaming users because a single connection can be used to transfer both voice and data.

Standards

The protocol that enables the transmission of multimedia (voice, data, and video) traffic over connectionless data networks such as IP networks and the Internet are the ITU H.320 and H.323 standards. H.320 provides support for conferencing over Integrated Services Digital Network (ISDN) connections; H.323 provides the same support over LAN connections. Both enable the establishment of voice and video calls over a TCP/IP network, and they provide for interoperability between vendor products. They also support data sharing using the ITU T.120 standard. H.320 and 323 mask the underlying physical infrastructure, so that communication can take place over high-capacity, wireless, or dial-up connections.

Another influential standard is the Microsoft Telephony Application Program Interface (TAPI). TAPI enables IP Telephony in the Microsoft Windows environment. It supports the H.323 standard and IP multicast conferencing, such as that provided by the Internet Multicast Backbone (MBONE), an experimental network built on top of the Internet for the broadcast of multimedia content. Novell provides a similar capability with the Telephony Services Application Protocol Interface (TSAPI).

The IP Telephony (iptel) working group of the IETF is leading other protocol development efforts. The group has set out to describe a call-processing syntax between the user and the underlying communications framework, a service model supported by the syntax, and a Gateway Attribute Distribution Protocol. This protocol will enable gateway devices to publish capabilities using descriptive attributes between capable platforms.

Role of the Directory

From a directory perspective, the major issue that IP Telephony raises is the conversion of source and destination information from a phone number to a network address. Figure 10.2 shows the technical evolution of this conversion.

Users have traditionally connected to another person over a voice network by entering a phone number consisting of a local number, perhaps an area or regional code, and maybe even country routing information. Users are adept at knowing whether a call is local, and they are familiar with dialing access numbers for outside lines, for intercompany networks, or for outside long distance.

If users make the same connection with IP Telephony, a major change is immediately apparent: The connection between points is accomplished using IP addresses instead of the numbers traditionally associated with people or companies. Users have to undergo a significant mapping effort to associate these traditional numbers to and from a network destination. For early adopters using IP Telephony, exchanging IP addresses was the standard route to establishing a connection. If IP Telephony is to be used by a broader audience with varying levels of technical expertise and technology tolerances, developers need to devise a mapping solution that masks the complexity of determining and using endpoint addresses. The directory is a logical choice as a tool to accomplish this objective.

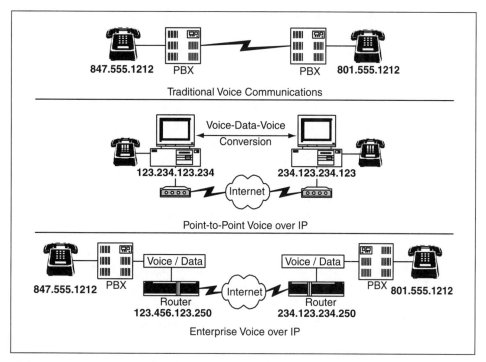

Figure 10.2   Traditional voice-to-network mapping.

Considerations

A number of products enable the transmission of voice traffic over the Internet. Using the Internet is a viable alternative to Plain Old Telephone Service (POTS), one that represents the potential to save large organizations significant amounts of money for long distance charges, but several issues make using the Internet as a voice backbone difficult today.

First of all, the Internet does not provide for deterministic paths or for Quality of Service. The result of this is that if one packet takes 30 milliseconds to be transferred and the next takes 200 due to some change in direction or capacity, the voice message may sound bouncy or jittery. These delays may also result in correspondents talking over each other. Products used for IP Telephony address these delays by buffering packets at each end of the link. These Quality of Service issues are being addressed at several levels, but they will not be completely resolved for some time.

In addition to the work discussed elsewhere in this book regarding the benefits offered by the Directory Enabled Networks initiative, there are also implementations of the IETF Resource Reservation Protocol (RSVP), which provides resource allocation on all of the network components between endpoints. Issues associated with capacity continue to represent a legitimate barrier to the use of the Internet as an alternative form of voice communications.

We have discussed Quality of Service initiatives and Directory Enabled Networks in detail in Chapter 7, "Network Management." The intent of these initiatives is to provide policy-based Class of Service based on the kind of traffic traversing the network. The directory is the repository for these policies, which must be implemented across all of the links associated with the information transfer, within or outside of the organization. DEN-capable hardware will begin reaching the market in the year 2000 timeframe, but end-to-end solutions may take several years to appear, particularly between organizations, carriers, and service providers. In the interim, implementers will be faced with the need to address quality issues with additional bandwidth and service-level agreements. Providers like AT&T, MCI Worldcom, PSInet, and GTE Internetworking will have to provide the Quality of Service capabilities and guarantees to meet these growing organizational initiatives.

Another issue is the quality of data sampling and compression. Voice over IP is a digital representation of an analog signal. Based on the level of sampling and the compression algorithms that are employed, the quality of the signal may not be as clear or as continuous as the analog or higher-quality digital signals that we are accustomed to with POTS and PBXs. The technology is improving rapidly, however, and the potential cost savings associated with it will help to focus attention on new research and solutions. Another form of traffic that will traverse the voice/data connection is facsimile. Although compression of fax data may be more efficient, tolerance for data/packet loss is effectively nil. On the other hand, the completion of a fax transmission is significantly less time-sensitive than voice traffic. Both voice and fax, however, underscore the need for the reliable throughput of information.

Where does this fit with the directory? Well, in traditional telephony, all that you required to contact someone else was that person's phone number, sometimes an area code, and, if it was an international call, some other series of codes corresponding to the topology in use in the destination country. Not always a simple proposition, but certainly one that is well understood. If all else fails, there is always information or an operator, who may even dial the number for you, for a fee.

With IP Telephony, even though there are similarities, the whole arrangement changes. First of all, with the growing use of the Dynamic Host Configuration Protocol, the number (or IP address) associated with an endpoint changes periodically, usually as frequently as a user logs on to the network. Second, firewalls may prevent the passage of voice traffic, or proxy servers may be employed to escort traffic past the firewall. There is also no notion of an operator per se. What is needed is a logical directory associated with the person you want to contact, in which the physical node address is constantly updated. This requires dynamic registration of addresses by the receiving node, provided that network barriers established on corporate or ISP boundaries allow for voice traffic.

An approach to this has been attempted with Internet Locator Services (ILS), such as the one provided by Microsoft and 411.com to support the use of data conferencing. The same issues apply to data conferencing as to IP Telephony. When a user loads the receiving software, the node address is registered on the ILS. It also signifies that the receiving node is available to accept incoming "calls." The net effect is that a dynamic and universally accessible directory is required within or between enterprises that enable individuals to locate each other, reflect associated policy requirements, and signify that they are available to communicate. Figure 10.3 shows how this environment might look.

Within large organizations that are looking to exploit the benefits of IP Telephony, this initiative underscores the need for a corporate directory. As the commercial solutions to enable acceptable-quality Internet telephony become viable, so too will the need for a directory capable of enabling its use.

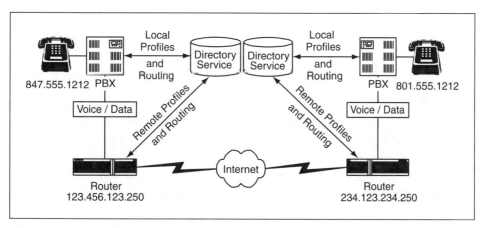

Figure 10.3   Introducing the directory to telephony and voice over IP.

Computer-Telephony Integration and the Universal Inbox

As we innovate with technology to fit our changing communications needs and lifestyles, more and more ways to exchange information are becoming important. Text paging is blurring with numeric paging; voice, text, paging, and faxes are blending with e-mail correspondence; portable telephones and other devices are being equipped with browsers and messaging clients. For years, as the number of alternative communications paths have grown, so has the desire to integrate and to simplify access to this correspondence. The ultimate goal is a single point of collection and access to all of the varied forms of communication that we might receive.

The kinds of devices being used to present correspondence to a recipient are changing rapidly. The domain of conventional terminal devices like personal computers is expanding to include the home television, and client technologies are moving more and more to highly functional Web browsers. To accommodate this, presentation and publication mechanisms are becoming more and more server oriented, particularly Web servers. The client paradigm has grown to include the portable telephone, the pager, personal digital assistants, and miniaturized personal computers, some with cellular or wireless capabilities for portable network access.

The capabilities of the single point of access, the universal inbox, are growing. Digital communications capabilities of the inbox include voice mail, voice-to-text and text-to-voice, call forwarding, fax receipt and forwarding, fax optical character recognition for text conversion, paging, text-to-paging, and a variety of vendor differentiating capabilities. In order to accomplish all of this conversion and distribution, the directory can play a key role as the clearinghouse for routing and forwarding, as well as the repository for profile information. As examples, consider that the recipient needs to identify the current receiving point. While traveling, the recipient may use a portable telephone, PDA, or pager. The receiving point will trigger the execution of conversion and forwarding rules, particularly which messages get forwarded and the format in which they will be presented. Other messages, of lower priority or from unselected recipients, may be left for retrieval by a PC-based client at a later time. How the directory is employed is a vendor or enterprise decision, but it is clear that a quantity of information about the recipient must be maintained that intersects with other personal and profiling characteristics of interest to the organization.

Video Conferencing

Video conferencing represents the ability to provide a point-to-point or multipoint meeting of participants in different locations. Video conferencing is used for training, meetings, and other business functions, and it is predicated on having relatively high-quality visual and audio links between locations. Usually, video conferences are conducted in specialized facilities that have cameras, microphones, television displays, and loudspeaker capabilities to provide a "nearly there" experience for participants. Participating in a video conference is much like a teleconference, with the addition of video capabilities. The benefit to participants is that video conferencing provides the ability to exchange visual as well as audio information and to experience the physical interaction between participants. Recent developments in the desktop environment utilize multimedia capabilities to enable a user to participate in a video conference without leaving the office.

Many large organizations, particularly those that are global, have video conferencing facilities throughout their enterprise. Video conferencing facilities are specialized. In addition to providing a comfortable meeting and working environment, they include all of the associated hardware and underlying communications links needed to establish and maintain a reliable session. They often have the ability to integrate whiteboards and computer presentations, and they offer copy stands and cameras for flat artwork or documents. Commercial ventures have also entered into the video conferencing arena, including telecommunications and other business services firms.

Role of the Directory

Video conferencing offers several opportunities for the use of directory services. Each facility has a number of profile components associated with it. These include the number of people that can be supported, the capabilities and manufacturer of the equipment available for use in the facility, hours of operation, location and directions to the facility, perhaps the cost of using the facility, and other related characteristics. Equally important are the communications details associated with the facility. Each facility has several connection options based on the connection mode in use (ISDN or LAN). Establishing a session is usually straightforward, but it often requires the initial support of a coordinator familiar with the equipment and the communications environment, particularly when communicating between companies, when using special bridging hardware, and other similar conditions. In these situations, the directory is a candidate for publishing information such as the voice and ISDN numbers for the site, the network address, troubleshooting number, and any specific connection characteristics associated with the facility. Manufacturers such as Intel and PictureTel are already incorporating the ability to publish and retrieve this information from directories that support LDAP access.

The capabilities of video conferencing are also being extended to the desktop. Developers such as Microsoft, Lotus, and others have incorporated video into their data conferencing tools. Microsoft has published a collaboration tool called NetMeeting, Lotus has published a similar tool called Sametime. Both support the use of LDAP directories to locate conference participants. The Sametime server comes with its own built-in directory service and is capable of using existing Domino directories. Microsoft provides a directory service for NetMeeting known as an Internet Locator Service, or ILS.

Summary

As organizations use the Internet as an alternative mechanism for carrying voice and multimedia, new ways to identify the location and characteristics of the endpoints, or clients, are needed. The traditional phonebook paradigm no longer applies. In its place, the directory is capable of maintaining the profiles and address information needed to establish an effective communications session between correspondents on the Internet, and it can be utilized by all of the associated resources needed to convert and transport the information between participants. Additional developments, such as multicasts, make it possible to do broadcasts to a number of recipients, and conferencing technologies make it realistic to share multiple kinds of information associated with a session to multiple participants in that session.

The directory also influences the location and conversion of information destined for a single entity. The notion of a universal inbox represents the consolidation of numerous technical solutions; the directory can act as the profiling mechanism that governs their interaction. Video conferencing represents another domain that will benefit from the consolidation of all the attributes needed to establish a session with a single or multiple locations in one place, particularly as the relationship between those locations becomes less distinct.

Meta-Directories

Earlier chapters helped you develop an appreciation for the broad range of issues that a directory can address, from address lists to support for authentication, digital signatures, and confidentiality in electronic transactions. One of the most compelling applications of directories across the enterprise, however, is the use of directory technology in the role of a *meta-directory*.

Before we explore meta-directories in detail, let's review the definition of a meta-directory. A meta-directory collects information about a single object or entity in one place. The information comes from a variety of sources; the meta-directory acts as a clearinghouse for other directories.

Multiple directories containing the same information about people and resources are expensive and prone to inaccuracy. The meta-directory approach is popular because it represents the information about entities and objects in a consistent way, simplifies the collection and distribution of the information throughout the organization, and can be employed to eventually reduce the number of single-purpose directories in an organization.

The reasons for developing a meta-directory are many and varied. An organization may be motivated to investigate meta-directories for both technical and business reasons. Some indicators that a meta-directory might be an appropriate solution are these:

- High network administration costs
- A constantly growing amount of redundant information within the organization
- The need to publish accurate information about a variety of resources for use by partners, customers, and third parties
- A mixed security environment with multiple directories supporting a variety of protocols and techniques

As communities of interest collect information from disparate sources to drive the formation of virtual enterprise networks, the need for directory integration and publishing is greatly increased.

This chapter discusses the role that a meta-directory can play in supporting business needs, the issues that must be addressed to develop a viable meta-directory solution, and some of the tools available to support a meta-directory implementation.

The History of Directory Consolidation

In the late 1980s and early 1990s, the proliferation of local area networks and LAN-based applications forced companies to invest in or develop tools for directory synchronization. Not only were directories proliferating, they shared a significant amount of common information and caused a similar rise in administrative costs. At the same time, the standards community was developing standards for directory services, and the vendor community was working to address similar issues with commercial products. One of the major drivers of directory synchronization was electronic mail synchronization, so that employees and partners could share information using this "booming new capability" between legacy and LAN applications. Many of the directory synchronization solutions that came to market were developed to resolve messaging-related issues.

Driven by Convergence

Three major mail environments of this era required interoperability. The first was the host and mainframe environment that served terminal users. The second was the community served by remote users, who received access to electronic mail using value-added networks like AT&T and service providers like CompuServe. The third was the LAN mail community, using products like cc:Mail or Network Courier. Making the data in these directories consistent seemed like a logical approach. We hadn't yet realized that the convergence of application functionality across disparate systems was introducing major issues in organizations.

Electronic mail addresses brought numerous issues with synchronization to light. A single individual would have an e-mail address for each e-mail system he or she might use. Each e-mail system had an associated directory, which contained information about the individual. Because the e-mail addresses were different, different routing information was required to get electronic mail delivered between different end systems. As a result, an organization needed synchronization tools to keep an X.400 address, an SMTP address, a Microsoft Mail address, and a PROFS address for each individual. In addition, each of the different application directories had to be populated so that the mail got delivered to the right end system based on the user's preference. Bringing all of these factors together required more than simple synchronization; data transformation logic was required as well.

The tools required for electronic mail synchronization stood in the middle of all the disparate systems. Some of the data transformation capabilities incorporated into the synchronization solutions served as the model for today's meta-directory products. The directory services technologies survive as well because several of the synchronization tools utilized X.500 as the common information repository, while others used relational databases.

A meta-directory serves as the focal point for several different, but logically related, information repositories. While the heritage of synchronization tools is based in e-mail, other networked applications, and operating system directories, today's meta-directory tools also include human resources, enterprise resource planning, relational databases, system management, and nearly every other repository imaginable.

Synchronization or Consolidation?

Why should an organization use a meta-directory? Arriving at the answer to this question involves considering many factors. Usually, an organization that asks this question is already tying together the information in several information repositories, like e-mail, collaboration, and NOS directories. Many of these environments already have rudimentary synchronization applications incorporated in them, and these work quite well for their intended use. The question becomes one of scale, that is, when does it become practical, or an imperative, to begin managing the information associated with an entity on a consolidated basis.

Usually, it becomes apparent that the information in multiple environments is not consistent or that information needs to be brought together in ways that require a major initiative. These initiatives also usually involve multiple data owners who are not accustomed to sharing or taking an enterprise view of the information. Data owners could include physical or system security, human resources, or third parties like insurance providers or financial institutions, to name a few. The more disparate the information is in purpose or function, and the greater the number of sources or users of information, the more likely it becomes that an intermediary view must be developed. This view often takes the form of a meta-directory.

You might ask, why don't I just buy a synchronization tool? Most of the synchronization capabilities that have survived in products today are embedded, such as the ability to synchronize the NOS directory with Lotus Notes. If these tools exist and address your needs adequately, then by all means—use them! Directory synchronization tools are generally point-to-point between applications, so don't expect to solve major synchronization issues between multiple applications with them.

Most of the companies that started out solving the synchronization problems in the early days have evolved into meta-directory solution providers. Some examples of these vendors include ISOCOR, Control Data Systems, Wingra Technologies, and Innosoft. Other vendors, such as WorldTalk and Boston Software Works, have disappeared from the directory market. Some vendors have merged, like ISOCOR with Netscape; others have been acquired, like Soft*Switch by Lotus and Zoomit by Microsoft. And there are newcomers to the market as well, including Siemens, Maxware, and IBM. Longer term, The Burton Group predicts that meta-directory capabilities will become inherent in all directory solutions, as the importance of being able to tie together disparate data sources becomes an integral requirement for organizations.

Four Perspectives on Meta-Directories

In its paper "Meta-Directory Functionality Revisited," published in 1998, The Burton Group identified four categories of meta-directory capabilities prevalent in the marketplace today:

- Single Administration Client
- Information Broker (passive and dynamic)
- Single-Solution Meta-Directory
- Meta-Directory Add-In

The Single Administration Client is really not a meta-directory; it provides a single point of administration into multiple directories. Like an integrated synchronization tool, the administration client provides limited utility. It allows an administrator to access multiple directories, but it doesn't provide any capability (other than the administrator) to ensure that a change applied to the information in one directory is applied to the information in another directory. The functionality is usually provided in a browser-like environment using common protocols like HTTP.

An Information Broker acts as an intermediary between a user and the information repository. The broker may be passive, as in situations where information like a telephone number is retrieved. It can also be dynamic, as in the case where a meta-directory acts a proxy or single sign-on agent. Brokering is an intensive process where the meta-directory acts as a pass-through agent. Due to all of the intermediate processing steps involved, brokering is often not the first choice when deciding whether to keep a copy of the information in the meta-directory. However, when interacting with other systems as a proxy agent, brokering may be the only way to get at remote information.

A Single-Solution Meta-Directory provides integrated functionality in conjunction with a repository like X.500 or an LDAP directory. Usually the repository is integral to the solution and may consist of proprietary capabilities to improve security or performance. This is the most common approach to meta-directory products today.

A Meta-Directory Add-In abstracts the functionality of the meta-directory from the repository, giving the customer the choice of several repository options. While not common, this capability allows the customer to distinguish the meta-directory logic from the underlying repository.

Meta-Directory Structure and Function

Before we discuss how a meta-directory is structured and the functions it provides, it's helpful to understand the principle behind a meta-directory's operation. The meta-directory concept is based on the relational algebra concept of the *join*. If you look at the example in Figure 11.1, you'll see two tables of information. Notice that the rows in both tables share a common attribute, *employee id*. Based on the common attribute, a join merges the tables and creates a new table. Each row in the new table contains data from both of the original tables as one row in the new table. Without the common attribute in the original tables, the join could not take place.

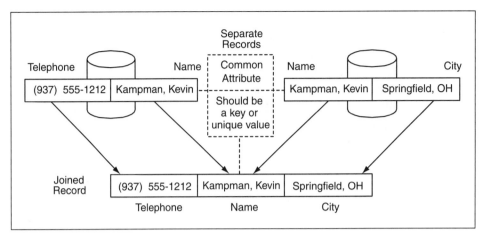

Figure 11.1   Join.

Keeping in mind this idea of taking data from more than one source and creating a definitive directory from it, let's talk about the structure and function of a meta-directory.

Meta-Directory Structure

What are the components of a meta-directory? First, a data repository is a key component of a meta-directory. The data repository can be either a directory or a database application; both can be seen in currently available products. The purpose of the data repository is to provide a place to maintain all of the information that is associated with each identity so that the identity information is consistent across the enterprise.

The second component of a meta-directory is a collection of applications. Applications can be grouped into two categories:

- Management and meta-directory administration.
- Software that collects and distributes information based on meta-directory information repositories. These applications are frequently called *connectors*.

What Functions Should a Meta-Directory Provide?

Before asking this question about the meta-directory, consider what functionality the underlying directory service should provide. The capabilities of the directory service, whether or not it is associated with a meta-directory, are to store information; provide support for the external access protocols and mechanisms, replication, and referrals; and support loading, backup, restoration, addition, deletion, and modification of the directory information. More sophisticated directory management tools provide capabilities like directory tree and schema structuring and alteration, transaction logging, and performance monitoring. A meta-directory provides additional capabilities based on this core set of services. Figure 11.2 provides an overview of the many ways in which a meta-directory can function in a networking environment.

Information Repository

The challenge for the meta-directory is to know where information about each identity resides and how to relate it to the identity. All of the repositories that are related to a meta-directory are known as *federated* directories. Two types of federated directories are associated with a meta-directory:

- Source repositories, known as the authoritative source or data of record.
- Destination repositories, which receive updates when the information at the authoritative source and the data in the meta-directory changes.

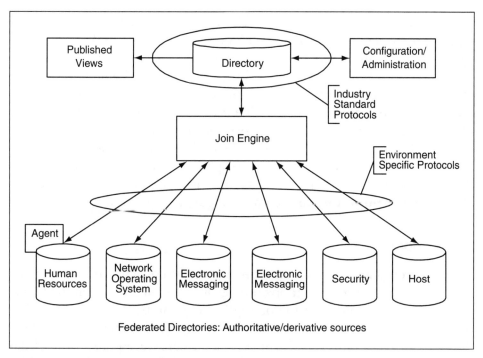

Figure 11.2   Meta-directory functions.

The meta-directory is the hub of the federated repositories. It contains the logic and rules that allow for the collection, transformation, and distribution of information within the entire system of repositories.

From an administrative perspective, the required functions are the ability to describe the structure of the information store in the meta-directory and the characteristics of the information. These characteristics include the joined record itself, as well as the source or owner, the destinations or dependents, and the data transformations that must occur to the information before it is stored or disseminated.

Keep in mind some special considerations about the meta-directory's information repository. Two distinct approaches may be used to gather the information in the meta-directory. One approach views the meta-directory as the working copy of all the information in the federated repositories. This condition arises because the information may not be otherwise readily accessible, or it may exist in a proprietary repository, or it may reside in a text file. In addition, security or communications capabilities may preclude direct access to the information. So, the needed information is collected in the meta-directory and used from that vantage point. The other possible approach to the meta-directory's information repository is that it stores no information at all—it only points to the needed information in the federated directories.

Some organizations isolate the meta-directory from production access. Others see the meta-directory as a shared repository and make it available for use by users and applications. Naturally, trade-offs exist with either approach. The advantage of the meta-directory being used only to propagate information to the production environment is that it can concentrate solely on making information consistent. If a problem occurs with the data, such as a failed feed from a source repository, the only impact on the production community is that the data is out of date for the period in question. The advantage of opening the meta-directory up to application and user access is that there is less redundancy. This may impact performance, however, and allows the meta-directory to become a single point of failure.

Applications

The other component of the meta-directory is the collection of applications that provide the communications linkage and the data between the federated directories. This collection of applications can be thought of as a *join engine*. To address the communications linkage requirements, an application may actually require its own dedicated hardware platform in situations where special communications links are needed. Today, however, the ubiquitous nature of TCP/IP makes establishing these connections less problematic. More and more, applications access repository information using this well-known and standard network protocol.

Once the underlying communications link is established, the situation gets more interesting. Some federated directories provide information to external environments, like the meta-directory, in text files. Others make access available using database protocols like Open Database Connectivity (ODBC) or Structured Query Language (SQL). Still other federated directories require the use of application program interfaces to extract information, particularly for applications like e-mail systems or network operating systems that have proprietary repositories. Fortunately, the proliferation of LDAP across many of these environments is simplifying access to information in much the same way that TCP/IP became the common denominator for networks.

The most significant development in meta-directory technology is the capability to detect changes in source repositories and trigger an update, first to the meta-directory itself, and then to the destination repositories. In order to accomplish this, monitors or agents for the meta-directory are installed on the source repositories. Every time a change is made to the source data, a trigger notifies the meta-directory, which initiates an update process. The processes that monitor source data rely on the capabilities of the management system supporting the information, and so they are not universally available. Older approaches often relied on batch updates using entire repositories or change files. So, while the more conventional approaches may still be necessary, the ability to provide near real-time updates to critical information with granularity at the attribute level makes it possible to realize capabilities like adding or suspending employee access to systems, based on conditions like hiring or termination.

How Do I Decide to Implement a Meta-Directory?

The decision whether to employ a meta-directory in an organization must be made based on many complex factors. Sometimes, organizations realize that they are developing custom applications around disparate information sources that accomplish the same objectives as a meta-directory. The desire to get away from the cost and maintenance associated with these applications is often the justification for acquiring a meta-directory. Other organizations realize that redundancy or inaccuracy is associated with critical business information, and they look to the meta-directory as a solution by using it to collect and distribute accurate information. Still other organizations are beginning to see the benefits associated with directory-enabled applications, and they recognize that in order to take advantage of these capabilities, a new method of bringing information together so that it can be accessed from a single source is required. Some of the initiatives that force this recognition include security applications and Web-based electronic business.

Organizations must address a number of questions as they assess the viability of a meta-directory solution in their environment. The next few sections discuss these questions in detail.

Do we as a community have control of the information we want to consolidate?

It is a noble goal to bring all of the information we would like to collect into a single source or repository. In reality, this is more of a social than a technical issue. Historically, the reason why information is distributed in so many different places in an organization is that it was placed there to address a single purpose or need. For example, the information in a Human Resources system is there to keep track of the background, performance, skills, and promotion history of individuals throughout their careers. There may or may not be any correspondence with other systems, such as payroll or physical security; usually these systems are distinct.

There are reasons for this isolation. First of all, automated systems for information management did not begin to appear on a regular basis in organizations until the mid-1960s. As solutions were developed, they were usually put together to meet a specific need. The notion of an integrated database system did not even appear until the late 1970s. And so, point solutions were developed and deployed asynchronously. Some of them are operational at the close of this century. Maybe the Year 2000 scare is a good thing if it forces organizations to implement integrated systems that break down this isolation between point solutions.

What is more difficult to deal with is that the functional isolation in organizations prevents the integration of information. Unless there is a business prerogative to use Human Resources information, for example, in the e-mail address list, it is often difficult to convince the HR group to provide access. The good news is that much of the HR information is out of date, and so "self-service" approaches to solicit updates from employees are becoming common. The use of the meta-directory to propagate these changes becomes compelling. Convincing all of the potential participants, or data owners, to participate in a meta-directory implementation is a formidable challenge unless there is a shared goal or objective. The identification of business drivers and the development of a strategy that has the blessing of senior management go a long way toward loosening the grip on information.

Do we have a management imperative? Is this a strategic or tactical initiative? How can I tell?

One of the common adages about management is that the language of management is money. For many people in information systems, the challenge of getting funding is the translation of a perceived technical need into perceived benefits to the organization. Is it going to reduce costs or improve efficiency, make the organization more competitive or allow it to leverage new markets? A thorough examination of these kinds of opportunities must be associated with any IT investment. A meta-directory implementation can do all of these things given the right governing principles and alignment with business objectives. Convincing management that it is the right thing to do is really more important than a detailed architecture initially because management support makes or breaks a project from the outset. The early objective then is to align the need for the technical solution in a big way with business drivers and objectives.

A meta-directory is a strategic investment that is often driven by tactical objectives. Meta-directories are often made as infrastructure investments to address pressing data integration objectives, such as e-mail and NOS directory integration. Over time, this integrated repository begins to enable strategic initiatives such as electronic business. It is useful to enumerate all of the areas that a meta-directory can enable or facilitate and to categorize those as strategic or tactical. A clearer perspective of the role that the meta-directory plays will result.

What kinds of organizations need this? Are there any that don't?

The meta-directory concept is exposing many new and interesting ways to manage organizational information. As with the directory, the technology is also becoming increasingly embedded in all network-enabled applications and services. Over time, the directory will become as commonplace as the operating system, and the meta-directory will be seen as a way to extend the reach of the directory. Not all organizations need this capability today; every organization of any size will need it in the future. The reach of the organization will extend to others, making ways to tie the information together an imperative for survival.

Are we doing this top down or bottom up?

There are so many possible data sources to integrate because organizations implemented solutions as they became available. The meta-directory is really a top-down solution in that it is intended to tie all of these disparate sources together. It may, and often is, implemented to address an immediate need, but it will achieve visibility as the usefulness and accuracy of organizational information grow. New opportunities will appear based on early successes, and so the need to plan for a bottom-up, top-down strategy is important.

Do we want to reduce the number of directories over time or just keep adding to the confusion?

A meta-directory is a major undertaking, and developing more tactical directories instead of attacking the issue head on is always a risk in an organization. This is the most critical issue facing organizations trying to determine whether to implement "yet another directory." The bigger issue, though, is the failure to develop a strategy for what the right direction is in any given situation. There are cases when developing a point solution is the only alternative, others where it is clearly the wrong thing to do. Developing guiding principles for the use of directory services in an organization is a basic necessity given the number of product solutions and the changing ways of doing business in the future.

Won't Active Directory or NetWare Directory Services or IBM SecureWay or [insert product name here] solve my directory problems?

Over the next three to five years, leading vendors will release a number of enterprise directory products. Directory awareness will be a basic element of almost every product that is network enabled, from network interface cards to operating systems. The issue here is not what product to use because many organizations will have all of them. The critical issue is understanding the role of the directory in the organization and having an overarching and adaptable strategy that incorporates new technologies as these become available.

Meta-Directory Design Issues

Meta-directories can provide significant benefits to an organization. To achieve these benefits, the organization has to be willing to make a major commitment throughout the enterprise to make a meta-directory work, with a lot of up-front thinking before implementation begins. This section presents the most critical design issues for meta-directory implementation.

IDs Required

Information in a meta-directory is organized around identities, or entities, that represent some real-world object. The basic assumption of the join is that for any two records brought together, some corresponding attribute or characteristic between the two records exists. In the real world, this is usually not the case, so some manner of retrofitting the data is required. Three approaches can be used to retrofit the data:

- Associate a unique identifier with the identity and then that apply identifier to all of the records related to the identity
- Develop mapping tables that identify the correspondence between records
- Use a combination of the two preceding methods

In a large organization with lots of information, implementing any of these approaches is a daunting task. Unfortunately, existing meta-directory products don't provide much help in addressing the issue of information correspondence. Even those products with algorithms and logic for identifying near matches require human intervention to complete the matching process. Although it seems quite simple on the surface, even the process of developing a unique identifier for an identity can be difficult. Finding an element of information that serves the purpose of linking records and that can always be associated with an identity is not an easy process. Care must be taken to prevent the information from being appropriated and used in ways that were not intended and to keep the identifier static. The best policy is to use a large integer value or alphanumeric string and expose it only for meta-directory purposes. The unique identifier can serve as the relative distinguished name (RDN) of the entry once it is placed in the directory.

Information Quality

Another issue that those who wish to implement meta-directories must face is the quality of information stored in individual directories. Very few of the organizations we've dealt with in the course of directory implementations have scrupulously maintained the information in all of the repositories in their organizations. Addresses and phone numbers change, certain data attributes become redundant or obsolete, and reporting relationships dissolve and re-form. Usually only the information that matters, such as payroll information, is kept up to date. So, in addition to finding ways to tie information together, organizations also have to address the issue of data cleansing.

Most of the effort required for meta-directory implementation focuses on data identification and data quality issues.

Data, Data Everywhere

Consider for a moment the types of information kept about people within an organization. If you are an employee, you have a record in the Human Resources system. You usually have a telephone listing, and you may have a badge or card that gives you access to the facility. Information about your training and skills may be maintained in a portfolio. Sometimes you might have a travel profile. If you work on a company site, there is usually a mail stop and building code associated with the office you occupy. If you are a virtual worker, then there is some way to route information and physical delivery items to you. We've identified six or seven sources of information, and we haven't even started talking about network or system access, let alone the applications that you use, much less your place in the organizational hierarchy. Company systems have a lot of information about you, and organizing it in a central repository can be a big challenge.

We've spent a lot of time discussing directory content, the need to prepare or clean data up prior to loading the directory, and the need to apply some form of identifier to ensure uniqueness and facilitate the "join" of information. Until now, the practical matter of identifying what information exists in an organization and how it is related has been ignored.

In reality, however, this is a critical issue for the design of an effective meta-directory solution. Having spent a recent weekend pulling together information from various Personal Information Managers, spreadsheets, text files, and the like to load my new Palm Pilot, I can assure you that this will become a back-breaking exercise for any organization contemplating their directory implementation. Fifteen years ago when I started using Borland's Traveling Sidekick to keep track of my business contacts, I thought I had the answer to my prayers. Today, I am putting it out to pasture as technology finally gets the upper hand.

One of my clients recently asked me how to prepare for the introduction of meta-directory technology. They hadn't been through the strategy, the architecture, the design, or the planning, but they recognize that the day is coming when they will need to introduce a meta-directory into their organization. My advice was to take an inventory of their current information repositories, including the content, identify the source data and owners, and consider how they would like to tie that information together to address redundancy and distribution of the information across the enterprise.

Knowing what you have and how you use or intend to use it is a major piece of any directory integration project. It assists you with finding the gaps between what you have and what you need, and it allows you to begin bringing the owners of the information together. Knowing that the same name and address information is entered and stored into 10 or 15 different systems and that only, maybe, one of them is right is a compelling example of redundancy. More compelling is the realization that it takes two to three weeks to make a new employee productive by giving him or her access to all of the needed systems. A clincher is that it may take just as long or longer to remove that access for a terminated employee. One of my previous employers took one year to remove me from the remote access and e-mail system, and then only at my request.

A number of software engineering tools on the market today are designed to provide diagrams of information models and transformations. For a simple directory project this may be excessive; a simple table showing name mappings between systems may suffice, along with a few data flow diagrams, developed in something like Visio or another graphics tool. Preparing a good graphical data mapping and data flow is an excellent approach to scoping the nature and extent of your meta-directory project. It will help identify the extent to which you will need to modify existing repositories or develop intermediate stores to pull the information together.

This will be very useful when you begin to develop a Request for Proposal for your directory vendor or systems integrator. The inventory, developed from a product-neutral perspective, will also make it easier to transition from one solution to another should that need arise, say, during or after a pilot test. For large projects, soliciting the assistance of a data librarian in your organization will help to simplify your efforts, especially with respect to information residing in legacy or heritage systems.

Another class of tools exists that may be valuable to you as you attempt information translation and conversion. Products like Monarch and Data Junction provide utilities to extract information from one source and convert it for use in another. Depending on the extent to which legacy or stand-alone data is an issue, these tools can also help with the data cleansing operations you will no doubt have to address.

Schema Design and Exchange

Like any database system, the directory is flexible and extensible enough to allow for the development of custom objects and attributes to meet the specific need of an organization. This flexibility raises issues for interoperability, however. Not knowing how an object is defined or represented is a significant barrier to an application developer from another organization who is trying to interface to your directory, and assumptions made by products like browsers may limit their ability to interpret customized schemas.

The IETF is attempting to address this in the LDAP protocol by use of a technique called schema publishing. This work is still in development, with the intent that an application could access a directory and interrogate it as to the structure of the schema, objects, and attributes, given the appropriate permissions. Today, it is common to rely on the use of well-understood objects and attributes to ensure some level of compatibility. For this reason, it is a good practice to examine existing work in the area of attribute and object definitions and to utilize these before creating custom objects. The use of inherited characteristics for objects is also a good practice, as many of the standard attributes can then be interpreted by the external application.

A promising development in the area of information exchange between directories is the recent interest in the use of the eXtensible Markup Language, or XML, to describe and to exchange information between directories. The need to replicate information between directories has been challenged by major vendors like Microsoft. They have stated that synchronization is more appropriate and viable. LDIF, the LDAP Data Interchange Format, provides a viable approach to the exchange of directory information in text format. XML, or DirXML, or the Directory Services Markup Language (DSML) initiatives may provide even more flexibility to describe and move information between directory services and between applications and directories.

Adopting a Center-of-the-Universe View

Directories are but one of the service capabilities being abstracted from the applications and infrastructure environment. These services include capabilities such as security, communications, and management. This approach is gaining favor as it allows developers to utilize a core set of enterprise applications and avoid having to redevelop each of these for each new initiative. It is important to recognize that these all support a set of services in their domain and that there are dependencies and overlap between the services, as we illustrate in Figure 11.3. For sharing common information between services, the directory is well positioned to be the core repository, having a well-understood set of access protocols and information model.

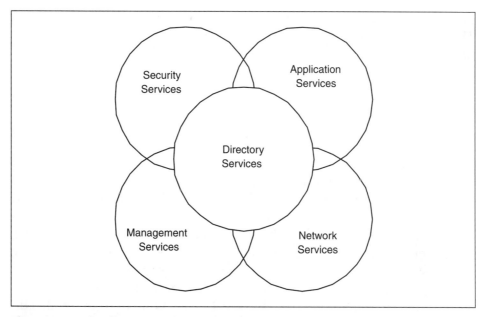

Figure 11.3 The directory as the core repository.

The directory is not, by itself, the solution to infrastructure issues. Using the core services capabilities in combination, however, helps to simplify the application development process and decrease the time needed to develop applications because the services interfaces are published and recognized, and extensible. Adaptations made for one purpose will help to simplify conditions for the next situation that arises.

For the services approach to be scalable, it must be generic and adaptable. Scalability comes from recognizing and eliminating restrictions and boundaries. The reason that TCP/IP is so widely accepted today is that it is a clear, relatively simple, and adaptable protocol. The core set of assumptions that went into the original protocol have withstood the test of time as IPv6 is being developed and released. Consider that extending the address space to accommodate more networked devices has not fundamentally broken earlier implementations as an indication that the original foundation of the protocol is sound.

In order for the services approach to truly scale, one of the boundaries that needs to be overcome is the issue of information ownership. We discussed this earlier in this chapter as an issue associated with the silo approach to systems implementation, such as human resources and payroll information being distinct and separate. There is always a bit of nervousness associated with handing the car keys over to a valet—sharing information is not always an easy thing. Organizations must come to accept that information is a corporate asset and not one that is tied to a functional area. The benefits of a single point of access for enterprise information are compelling in response to the need for agility and flexibility in the development community.

Summary

The development and implementation of a meta-directory solution has social and technological facets that need to be addressed. The information that is used to populate the meta-directory, and the repositories that the meta-directory is used to populate, represent organizational conventions and perspectives that need to be addressed from a project perspective. Ownership of the information needs to be elevated to an enterprise level; control should be maintained at the authoritative source.

Meta-directory functionality today can be provided in several different ways, by an administrative client, by directory add-ons, or by integrated directory and meta-directory solutions. Over time, as the value and necessity of meta-directories are recognized, they will become integral to all directory solutions.

The success of a meta-directory implementation will rely on proper scoping, management, and organizational support. Understanding where data resides, who controls it, and where similar information is needed is a complex exercise that must be completed in order to understand the type of solution needed. In order to publish the information in the directory, the information will need to be mapped to standard or custom objects and attributes. The standards community is working diligently to make the publishing of information between organizations meaningful and productive.

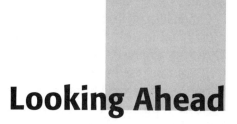

Looking Ahead

The directory marketplace is growing rapidly as the networked computing community discovers new applications for directory technologies. This growth is being driven by the maturity of client/server and network computing, by the need to manage potentially redundant information, and by pressure to reduce the costs of administration. The consolidation of information in the directory is driving the investigation and implementation of meta-directory technologies to distill disparate directory information into an enterprise or a community-of-interest view. This chapter presents an overview of emerging trends in directory technologies and their outlook for the future.

From Isolation to Interoperability

Directory technology may be nearly ubiquitous, but it is only today that it is starting to become interoperable. The recognition of the need for more general-purpose directory services offerings, as opposed to application-specific or embedded solutions, is fueling new interest in the directory technology market. The lack of practical standards for interoperability in the early phases of directory development led to many proprietary solutions. Until work began on X.500, and later LDAP, an accepted standard for embedded directories did not exist, so developers created what they needed to get the job done. Notable implementations of the move from specific to general-purpose directories include Novell's Bindery evolving into Novell Directory Services (NDS), and Banyan's StreetTalk evolving from a specific solution to a cross-platform integration method. Other implementations are less well known but serve similar application requirements. NDS is one of the first "X.500-like" solutions to achieve widespread recognition.

Other, less well-known directories are being integrated into the fold. The most notable include Dynamic DNS and DHCP, as well as the developing Directory Enabled Networks (DEN) initiative. The DEN initiative is an activity of the Distributed Management Task Force (DMTF). It is intended to allow organizations to manage their networks using directory services as the core repository for information about networked devices and their relationships. Once these objects are identified in the directory, the information can be used to govern the devices using management policies. Typical uses would be to support chargeback, quality of service, and network security. The DMTF is also developing the Common Information Model (CIM) for the directory that will be used as a framework for characterizing these resources. CIM includes information about persons, devices, applications, locations, protocols, media, services, policies, and profiles.

The growth of secure networking, in conjunction with the success of the Internet, is also having an influence on the directory marketplace, fueling the rise in popularity of secure remote access and Virtual Private Network solutions.

Standards versus Market Pressures

X.500, while a seminal influence on the market, failed to achieve widespread market acceptance due to its complexity and the perception of an incomplete feature set. To the uninitiated, X.500 is still incomplete. In reality, X.500 is more a work in progress as efforts to improve its scalability, interoperability, and security features continue. Starting with its first implementation, X.500 continues to break new ground with each iteration of the standard. Each success exposes new opportunities to refine its capabilities. For example, the notion of Certificate Revocation Lists in X.509 is an example of a solution to a problem, but in reality, until we knew we had the problem, we didn't know how complex the solution needed to be. Regardless of its detractors, X.500 is either the model or the production engine behind every commercial directory service offering. Even IBM has shipped a production X.500 directory to support its electronic business initiatives.

As far as the marketplace is concerned, a different view of directories has developed. The Lightweight Directory Access Protocol (LDAP) has won out over other solutions as the standard for access and interoperability. Most production directories in use or being released support the LDAP standard as an access mechanism. All support LDAP version 2, and most are converging on support for LDAP version 3. For the repository, customers have a choice of X.500 or a variant; for access, LDAP is the standard. What will distinguish products in the developing marketplace will be scalability, ease of access and management, and developer and customer recognition. Characteristics like standards compliance will become the baseline.

Industry analysts foresee a time when there is only one logical directory in an enterprise. This nirvana will come about only after the expenditure of significant effort and resources to identify the current directory populations in the organization, address the common needs, consolidate the information, change the point of focus of the using community, and sunset the legacy systems. This transition will vary for many organizations, and it will last several to many years, based on the number of embedded directories and the strength of the commitment for consolidated repositories.

The marketplace will help to fuel the transition. The release of Active Directory with Microsoft Windows 2000 and the current Novell Directory Services community will both position organizations for directory consolidation. The application communities residing on mainframe and midrange platforms will also play a leading role, particularly as the need to access information in Internet time becomes more common. It will become a critical success factor, for example, for Web-based initiatives to be able to access a consolidated index of customer information in order to develop a tailored or customized page and profile for each customer dynamically. If each initiative develops its own repository and set of applications for each application, the redundancy could be enormous, not to mention the potential lack of consistency.

As we can see, both top-down (or application-driven) and bottom-up (or infrastructure-driven) factors influence the use of directories across the enterprise. The major issue in directory implementation is how to architect and utilize these repositories in a common and consistent manner. Standards represent some level of assurance that the strategy developed by an organization will be viable, but standards are not a panacea. As technology progresses and business needs change, standards adapt to keep pace. Adoption of a standard is a subscription to an approach; it is highly likely that the approach will evolve and change. The benefit is that it will (we hope) meet the needs of a larger community of vendors and users.

Business Drivers

The structure and operation of business enterprises are changing rapidly as the new century unfolds. Even without the influence of the Internet and the sideshow called Y2K, supply-chain integration and just-in-time manufacturing, as well as outsourcing and the extended enterprise, provide critical imperatives to reexamine the way we structure and use information. All of these are driven by the need to reduce costs and increase efficiency and productivity. The bad news about reducing costs and increasing efficiency and productivity is that organizations don't change the way they do things overnight, and in fact, they may not be able to change at all. The investments required may be too great. Some organizations cope by selling out, by acquisitions and mergers, or they just fade away. Those that survive, even those that do so by joining forces with another organization, will continue to face the need to manage information more effectively.

One of the most basic business issues that organizations face is the need to locate people and resources. People and resources can include local and enterprise information, and, in the case of the supply chain, the people and resources in partner organizations. This information exists in human resources systems as well as security systems, networks, application databases, manufacturing, and enterprise resource planning systems, to name a few. Large organizations often develop an enterprise view of this information, but the intent is driven by the need to consolidate information across several large systems, not necessarily to improve access or usability of the information.

Once we introduce the concept of an extended enterprise or community of interest, the scope becomes enormous for all of the participants. Not only do they need to have a solid understanding of their own environment, the need now exists for some common capability for information sharing among all of the organizations. Keep in mind that the luxury of doing this at a normal pace is just that, a luxury. The winners and survivors are those who do so at a competitive pace. The imperative that supply-chain management imposes on organizations is to be able to integrate people and processes with organizations outside of your own. Initiatives like the ISO-9000 standards, which quantify the quality of processes in an organization so that they are repeatable and can be measured by others, represents one example of how organizations are blending and exposing their processes and procedures from an interenterprise perspective.

Efforts to share directory information between enterprises are just beginning to surface. Organizations are beginning to share directory lists for the exchange of messages and for collaboration. Initiatives are beginning in communities of interest like the energy, automotive, and financial and insurance industries that are driving this to a higher level. For example, efforts are underway at the Automotive Industry Action Group to develop a common schema and Directory Service for the automotive industry. This initiative is in response to the success of the Automotive Network Exchange (ANX), an industry extranet intended to provide secure and high-performance Virtual Private Network services between automotive manufacturers and suppliers. The ANX network is based on the IPSec protocols for authentication and encryption. IPSec utilizes digital certificates to establish network relationships and to ensure the confidentiality of information. Initially, directory services will be utilized to support the exchange of these certificates. Over time, the need to publish an industry directory to locate information about resources in organizations will be required to support electronic commerce applications.

The Network Applications Consortium (NAC), which authored the Lightweight Internet Person Schema (LIPS), also has initiatives for information sharing underway. The NAC sponsors activities for its membership that will enable the cross-organizational sharing of directory information using a common schema.

A major issue raised by the need to share industry or supply-chain information on a global scale is the provision for platforms that will host the information. In addition to the need to characterize the information in a manner that is meaningful to all of the participants (the schema), the publishing requirement raises many issues. Is there a central access point that refers inquiries to participating directories? Should there be a meta-directory that publishes some set of information gathered from each of the subscribers? How can small entities that have little or no information technology infrastructure make their information known? Who owns and provides the platforms? Who makes sure that the information is reliable, accurate, and up to date? How are international requirements about the publishing of directory information satisfied? These and many other issues are on the table at industry organizations today.

Even though the notion that bringing all of this information together into one organizational or interenterprise directory service is compelling, the fact remains that in all organizations, the information we speak of resides in different locations and was established there to satisfy specific, rather than general, purposes. To complicate matters, the information is rarely up to date. In addition, because the data stores were established for specific purposes, there is often no mechanism in place to relate the information in one repository to the information in another. Even if there is some mechanism, it may be ambiguous, based on something like names. Usually, organizations must establish a Unique Identifier, or key, for every entity they would like to place in the directory and propagate this to all of the data stores containing information about that entity that will participate. Where this is not possible, the development of data mapping tables or other more cumbersome efforts may be required. Organizations should plan to address a major data integration and cleansing effort as they tie together this information to meet general needs.

Organizations also need to address what technologies they will employ to develop and maintain this information. The beauty of LDAP is that it is supported by almost every major repository technology available. This doesn't mean, however, that LDAP has been, or will ever be, retrofitted to earlier technologies. In addition, some information doesn't exist in a form that is suitable for direct integration, for example, flat text files or data embedded in application systems like PBXs. Most organizations, even those that have created their own solution for information integration using technologies like relational databases, have learned that X.500 and LDAP-based directories are best suited for directory integration and publishing. The strategic decision to adopt interoperable directory standards and technologies will need to be made by all organizations. It is a strategy that must be carefully examined, in terms of the impact on legacy environments as well as the capabilities required in the future. Efforts by database manufacturers to adopt standards for exchanging information will have a major influence on this business and technology direction. Compatibility and ubiquity will be key to the success of the solution over time.

The specific uses and general objectives for the directory in an organization will need to be catalogued and understood. The information model will be patterned, to a large extent, on these requirements. Access to the directory will be required for custom applications using published application program interfaces, in addition to today's well-known clients like electronic mail address lookups, Web browsers, and directory-specific clients (directory user agents) such as network management systems and remote access clients. As an organization examines the distribution of directory information across the enterprise, it will also need to address the distribution of management responsibilities. Initially the ownership of the information will remain with the authoritative source, but this may change as processes and procedures are improved. A commitment must be made to keeping the included information current, either by requiring end users to post updates (self-service) or by developing new processes and procedures to maintain the information. If there is no guarantee that the information can be kept accurate and up to date, its presence and value to the organization should be questioned.

Another category rapidly gaining dominance is the area of *single sign-on*, or a single authentication and access mechanism to multiple system resources. The complexity of today's automation environment, where a user needs to access multiple systems for multiple purposes, each with its own access requirements, is creating major security issues for organizations. In response, solutions are being developed that act as a single point of authentication for access to these systems. In many cases, the single sign-on solution acts as a proxy for the authenticated user to access other systems. The directory plays a role in profiling the user, identifying accessible networks and systems, and maintaining information required to provide access. It remains to be seen if organizations ultimately settle on one or several sign-on solutions, but it is clearly another security and productivity opportunity.

As organizations strive to reduce the cost of administration, one of the major opportunity areas is the use of multiple repositories to maintain similar information. Studies have shown that in large organizations, redundant directory data stores for employees number from 15 into the low 100s. Given that discrete administration processes are associated with each of these, the opportunity for the consolidation of information and processes is compelling. These studies address only workforce information. Other analysis indicates that for customers and trading partners, similar levels of redundancy exist. A detailed cost assessment usually exposes that the real cost of administering distributed directory information today can be reduced significantly by consolidation of these efforts to fewer or a single central repository over time. Real benefits are associated with a single point of access and with the ability to integrate manual and automated processes to respond to events using information located in the directory, such as the hiring, reassignment, and termination of employees. Other organizations have derived real benefits from being able to identify the entire workforce population (employees, contractors, business and trading partners) in a single repository.

The primary business driver for interorganizational networks like ANX is the need to reduce communications costs. In the past, companies utilized value-added networks (VAN) from companies like AT&T, Harbinger, and IBM to pass Electronic Data Interchange (EDI) documents. Based on highly structured relationships between the endpoints and the dedicated communications links provided by the communications carriers, there was rarely any question about the authenticity or security of information shared between organizations. The cost of transferring transactions in this environment is a detractor, however.

On the surface, the perceived cost of handling these transactions over VANs is fairly expensive in comparison to public network services like the Internet. Organizations have determined that by enabling secure communications over the Internet and private IP-based networks, they can realize significant cost savings for EDI and other forms of correspondence, such as secure electronic messaging. To accomplish this in a secure manner, public key-based capabilities such as digital signatures and encryption are employed. To be scalable, directory services are required to support an enterprise or interenterprise Public Key Infrastructure to manage certificates. Governments, industries, and organizations are investigating building their own infrastructures. At the same time, financial institutions, like the Bank of America and Zions Bank's Digital Signature Trust, and commercial concerns, like GTE Cybertrust, Thawte, and VeriSign, are building PKI capabilities to support electronic commerce. The U.S. government is helping by providing legislation as well as practical implementations of PKI to support the legitimacy and viability of digital signatures for electronic commerce purposes.

The ability to utilize public key capabilities is surfacing in other areas besides EDI. Organizations that support remote access to their networks by employees, contractors, and trading partners are beginning to employ public-key-based authentication and authorization. Vendors like Novell, Netscape, and Microsoft are providing support by incorporating public-key management tools in their products today. Storing and serving up the keys is only part of the problem.

A public key infrastructure (PKI) represents a set of social, legal, and operational responsibilities, processes, and procedures that insure that the information is legitimate and that the relationships represented by and between PKIs are trustworthy. Figure 12.1 shows the many relationships managed by a PKI.

The directory services solution employed to manage public keys can affect the performance and reliability of the PKI system. The directory is used to store the certificates as well as Certificate Revocation Lists (CRL), which identify certificates that have been revoked before they expire. There are

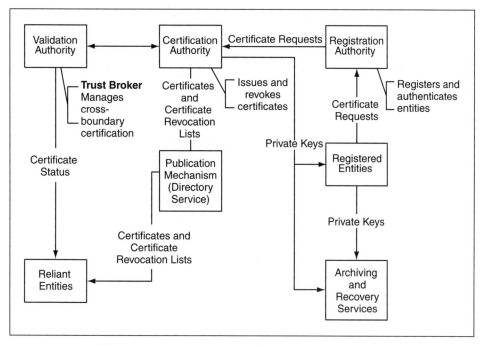

Figure 12.1 Public key infrastructure.

questions about the scalability of CRLs, as these are updated only periodically and may not reflect the status of the certificate in real time, particularly when this information is replicated between directories. Another approach to verifying the validity of certificates is On Line Certificate Status, where the status of a particular certificate can be verified. Protocol work is being done in this area, and the maturity of both approaches is improving.

The World Wide Web is having a significant influence on the nature of electronic commerce. EDI is a business-to-business approach for electronic commerce. The alternative, and what most analysts see as the bigger market, is business-to-consumer electronic commerce. Whether business-to-business or business-to-consumer, the ubiquity of the Web and browser technology makes this a fertile field for the development of technologies that will become the eventual replacement for EDI, in addition to presenting an interactive customer interface. For example, considerable attention is being given to the development of the Extensible Markup Language (XML), which will provide similar transaction modeling capabilities to those offered by the ANSI and UN/EDIFACT EDI transaction sets, on a highly customizable basis. XML provides the capability to develop any variety of identifiers, or tags, and declarations that represent the character-istics of the information content. The benefit of XML is that these can be de-veloped to meet specific purposes, dynamically. As these proliferate, the need to publish profiles that identify their purpose in a central repository grows—this offers another role for the directory.

Another recent development in the XML area is the development of di-rectory interchange standards around XML. This version of XML is called the Directory Services Markup Language (DSML). DSML promises to provide a common, cross-platform schema publishing and information exchange model that will help to tie directories together and simplify the process of integration. DSML also promises to make directory informa-tion available and meaningful in nondirectory environments, such as in browsers using HTML. DSML will augment the capabilities of LDAP and fill in some perceived gaps such as schema exchange and interpretation. It may also provide an alternative to LDIF, the LDAP data interchange standard.

At the Catalyst '99 conference, held at Lake Tahoe in July 1999, the Di-rectory Services Markup Language (DSML) Working Group was an-nounced. The group included representatives from Bowstreet, Novell, IBM, Oracle, the Sun-Netscape Alliance, and Microsoft. The first objective of the group is likely to be the development of a public standards proposal that will define a lowest-common-denominator set of Bowstreet's initial DSML implementation.

At the same conference, Novell also announced a product that works in conjunction with NDS that incorporates XML and the directory, called DirXML. Novell's approach is to utilize DSML as the foundation for a meta-directory solution that ties together multiple repositories in the enterprise using a common template and data description model. DirXML will enable views of non-NDS information to be incorporated into the NDS environ-ment. Using XML style sheets (XSLT) or templates, information can be de-scribed and made available to external applications from within NDS and described to develop NDS views as well.

We have discussed a variety of business drivers and application solu-tions that are appearing in the directory space. Today, organizations have a number of directories in place serving specific purposes. New applications for the directory are being identified, and major directory initiatives are un-derway in the software and hardware communities. For large organiza-tions, one of the biggest challenges will be to develop and adopt an enter-prise strategy for the use of directory services. The existence of so many directories represents the potential for redundant information, while managing and maintaining all of the directories represent significant redundant costs. These cost impacts extend through the application development and user communities, where seeking information in a distributed environment may be problematic, and worse still, may result in the retrieval of wrong or inaccurate information.

The Role of the Meta-Directory

Bringing all of this information together with a common focus is the intended role of the meta-directory. Meta-directory technologies exist today that tie together disparate applications directories and other, more rudimentary information sources so that all of the information about a particular entity in the organization can be presented as a join of that information.

The most common meta-directory approach today represents a set of services that connect to the distributed information sources, pull and push information to those sources, maintain a common repository of information or pointers to information sources, and maintain a profile about each entity being managed. This profile includes information such as the authoritative source for each attribute, the owner of the information, access rights, any transformations that are applied to the information when pulled or pushed between sources, frequency of updates, and distribution locations. Among the major vendors providing meta-directory applications today are Control Data Systems, IBM, ISOCOR, Siemens, Netscape, and Zoomit.

Meta-directory technology has a large heritage in directory synchronization tools. The best-known applications for directory synchronization were and are used to bring together the directories in applications like network operating systems, electronic mail, groupware, scheduling, and others. The impetus for their development was the rapid proliferation of these applications along with local area networks and distributed computing. See Figure 12.2 for the typical functions affected by directory synchronization.

What distinguishes meta-directories from synchronization tools is the meta-directory's enterprise approach to information management, as shown in Figure 12.3. Meta-directories have the ability to adapt to multiple environments and applications, to incorporate business rules and transformation logic into the information management process, and to serve as a centralized store for directory information using standards-based access protocols.

Long-term strategies for meta-directories often include the potential to displace distributed directories with a meta-directory information store.

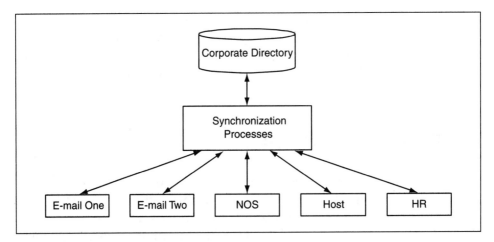

Figure 12.2   Directory synchronization.

Figure 12.4 shows some of the potential benefits of a meta-directory in the enterprise. This approach provides organizations the ability to isolate information from applications, a key services-based requirement for scalability and flexibility. A meta-directory information store also helps to protect an organization's investment in the collection and management of directory information because the directory is based on recognized standards for storage and access. As organizations expand, contract, and interact, the ability to publish and manage this resource information to meet changing business needs is critical.

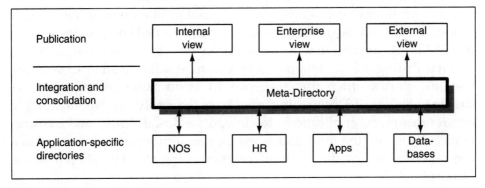

Figure 12.3   Meta-directory integration.

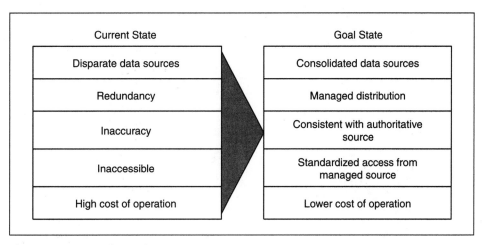

Current State	Goal State
Disparate data sources	Consolidated data sources
Redundancy	Managed distribution
Inaccuracy	Consistent with authoritative source
Inaccessible	Standardized access from managed source
High cost of operation	Lower cost of operation

Figure 12.4 Transformation.

Summary

Many compelling business drivers suggest the use of centralized directories in organizations. Organizations are challenged to share information about individuals and organizational roles and capabilities with other organizations, as global enterprises become more common. At the same time, the proliferation of numerous application-specific directories presents the opportunity to reduce redundant information and the management infrastructure required for maintaining that information. A major business driver for the sharing of information between individuals and organizations is Public Key Infrastructure, which provides a mechanism to share security information to enable electronic commerce.

Many of the approaches for bringing this information together are new. The good news is that the underlying mechanisms for information publishing and management are based on proven technologies and standards. Although they aren't perfect, the industry focus on standards-based solutions ensures that an organization's investments in best practices and procedures will be protected.

Acronym Listing

ACL   Access Control List

AD   Active Directory

ADO   ActiveX Data Object

ADSI   Active Directory Services Interface

AH   Authentication Header

ANX   Automotive Network Exchange

API   Application Program Interface

ASCII   American Standard Code for Information Interchange

ASN   Abstract Syntax Notation

BDC   Backup Domain Controller

BIND   Berkeley Internet Name Domain

CA   Certification Authority

CCITT   Consultative Committee for International Telephony and Telegraphy

CDS   Cell Directory Service

CHAP   Challenge Handshake Authentication Protocol

CIM   Common Information Model

CMIP   Common Management Information Protocol

CN   Common Name

COPS   Common Open Policy Service

CoS   Class of Service

CPS   Certificate Practice Statement

CRL   Certificate Revocation List

DAP   Directory Access Protocol

DARPA   Defense Advanced Research Projects Agency

DCE   Distributed Computing Environment

DDNS   Dynamic Domain Name System

DEN   Directory Enabled Network

DES   Data Encryption Standard

DHCP   Dynamic Host Configuration Protocol

DIB   Directory Information Base

DirXML   Directory Extensible Markup Language

DISP   Directory Information Shadowing Protocol

DIT   Directory Information Tree

DMD   Directory Management Domain

DMTF   Distributed Management Task Force

DN   Distinguished Name

DNS   Domain Name System

DOP   Directory Operational Binding Management Protocol

DSA   Directory System Agent

DSML   Directory Services Markup Language

DSP   Directory System Protocol

DSS   Digital Signature Standard

DUA   Directory User Agent

EDI   Electronic Data Interchange

ESP   Encapsulating Security Payload

FTP   File Transfer Protocol

GDS   Global Directory Service

HTML   Hypertext Markup Language

HTTP   Hypertext Transfer Protocol

IAB   Internet Activities Board

IDEA   International Data Encryption Algorithm

IESG   Internet Engineering Steering Group

IETF   Internet Engineering Task Force

IIOP   Internet Inter-ORB Protocol

IKE   Internet Key Exchange

ILS   Internet Locator Service

IMAP   Internet Message Applications Protocol

InterNIC   Internet Network Information Center

IP   Internet Protocol

IPSec   Internet Protocol Security

IPX   Internet Packet Exchange

IRC   Internet Relay Chat

ISAKMP   Internet Security Association and Key Management Protocol

ISDN   Integrated Services Digital Network

ISOC   Internet Society

IT   Information Technology

ITU   International Telecommunications Union

JNDI   Java Naming and Directory Interface

L2TP   Layer Two Tunneling Protocol

LAN   Local Area Network

LDAP   Lightweight Directory Access Protocol

LDIF   LDAP Data Interchange Format

LIPS   Lightweight Internet Person Schema

MAPI   Mail Application Program Interface

MBONE   Multicast Backbone

MD5   Message Digest 5

MHS   Message Handling Service

MIB   Management Information Base

MIME   Multipurpose Internet Mail Extension

MS   Message Store

MS-CHAP   Microsoft Challenge Handshake Authentication Protocol

MTA   Message Transfer Agent

NAC   Network Applications Consortium

NDS   Novell Directory Services

NIS   Network Information Services

NNTP   Network News Transfer Protocol

NOS   Network Operating System

NT   New Technology

NTAS   New Technology Advanced Server

OCSP   On-line Certificate Status Protocol

ODBC   Open Database Connectivity

OID   Object Identifier

OLE   Object Linking and Embedding

OLE DB   Object Linking and Embedding for Databases

ORB   Object Request Broker

OSI   Open System Interconnection

PAP   Password Authentication Protocol

PBX   Private Branch Exchange

PDC   Primary Domain Controller

PEM   Privacy Enhanced Messaging

PGP   Pretty Good Privacy

PIN   Personal Identification Number

PKCS   Public Key Cryptography Standard

PKI   Public Key Infrastructure

POTS   Plain Old Telephone Service

PPP   Point to Point Protocol

PPTP   Point to Point Tunneling Protocol

QoS   Quality of Service

RA   Registration Authority

RACF   Resource Access Control Facility

RADIUS   Remote Authentication Dial-In User Service

RC2   Rivest Cipher 2

RC4   Rivest Cipher 4

RDN   Relative Distinguished Name

RFC   Request for Comment

RMON   Remote Network Monitoring

RPC   Remote Procedure Call

RSA   Rivest-Shamir-Adelman

RSVP   Resource Reservation Setup Protocol

SA   Security Association

SAM   Security Accounts Manager

SASL   Simple Authentication and Security Layer

SET   Secure Electronic Transactions

SHA   Secure Hash Algorithm

S-HTTP   Secure Hypertext Transfer Protocol

SID   Security Identifier

SLP   Service Locating Protocol

S/MIME   Secure Multipurpose Internet Message Extension

SMTP   Simple Mail Transfer Protocol

SNA   Systems Network Architecture

SNADS   Systems Network Architecture Distribution Services

SNMP   Simple Network Management Protocol

SQL   Structured Query Language

SSL   Secure Sockets Layer

SSL/TLS   Secure Sockets Layer/Transport Layer Security

STDA   StreetTalk Directory Assistance

TAPI   Telephony Application Program Interface

TCP   Transmission Control Protocol

TCP/IP   Transmission Control Protocol/Internet Protocol

TGS   Ticket Granting Server

TGT   Ticket Granting Ticket

TLS   Transport Layer Security

TSAPI   Telephony Services Application Program Interface

UDP   User Datagram Protocol

VAN   Value Added Network

VLAN   Virtual Local Area Network

VoIP   Voice over Internet Protocol

VPN   Virtual Private Network

WINS   Windows Internet Naming Service

XDS   X/Open Group Directory Service

XML   Extensible Markup Language

Resources

Books

Comer, Douglas E. 1991. *Internetworking with TCP/IP*, Vol. I. Englewood Cliffs, NJ: Prentice Hall.

Ferguson, Paul and Geoff Huston. 1998. *Quality of Service: Delivering Quality of Service on the Internet and in Corporate Networks*. New York: John Wiley & Sons, Inc.

Gollman, Dieter. 1999. *Computer Security*. New York: John Wiley & Sons, Inc.

Howes, Tim and Mark Smith. 1997. *LDAP: Programming Directory-Enabled Applications with Lightweight Directory Access Protocol*. Indianapolis: Macmillan Technical Publishers.

Jain, Bijendra N. and Ashok K. Agrawale. 1993. *Open Systems Interconnection*, rev. ed. New York: McGraw-Hill, Inc.

Kearns, David and Brian Iverson. 1998. *The Complete Guide to Novell Directory Services*. San Francisco: SYBEX.

Kosiur, Dave. 1998. *Building and Managing Virtual Private Networks*. New York: John Wiley & Sons, Inc.

Minoli, Daniel and Emma Minoli. 1998. *Delivering Voice over IP Networks.* New York: John Wiley & Sons, Inc.

Naugle, Matthew. 1999. *Illustrated TCP/IP.* New York: John Wiley & Sons, Inc.

Plattner, B., C. Lanz, H. Lubich, M. Muller, and T. Walter. 1991. *X.400 Message Handling Standards, Internetworking, Applications.* New York: Addison-Wesley Publishing Co.

Radicati, Sara. 1994. *X.500 Directory Services: Technology and Deployment.* Boston: International Thomson Computer Press.

Schneier, Bruce. 1996. *Applied Cryptography,* 2d ed. New York: John Wiley & Sons, Inc.

White Papers

Lewis, Jamie and Daniel Blum. 1998. *Meta-Directory Functionality Revisited.* Salt Lake City, UT: The Burton Group.

Microsoft Windows 2000 Server Active Directory Technical Summary. 1999. Redmond, WA: Microsoft Corporation.

Mine, Hilary. 1998. *The Future of Online Communication.* Cedar Knolls, NJ: Probe Research, Inc.

Articles

Anonymous. "Coping with Coexistence: Strategies for Managing Multiple Directories." *InfoWorld* 19(46): 184.

Blum, Daniel. "For Directory Planners, The Name is the Game." *Network World* 15(38): 40.

Bruno, Lee. "Directory Services Tie It All Together." *Data Communications* March 1997: 74–83. www.data.com.

Burns, Christine. "Meta Directory Market Dawdles." *Network World* 14(47): 25.

Byrne, Donal and Cuneyt Ozveren. "Crafting the Directory-Enabled Network." *Network World* 15(11): 39.

Cox, John. "Vendors Embracing Directories as Key Net Technology." *Network World* 15(19): 8.

Duffy, Jim. "Directories to the Rescue." *Network World* 14(33): 30.

Fawcett, Neil. "The Direct Approach." *Computer Weekly* March 13, 1997: 42.

Gaskin, James E. "Directory Services—Think Beyond Your Network." *Business Communications Review* 27(12): 36–38.

Howes, Tim. "LDAP: Use as Directed." *Data Communications* February 1999: 95–104. www.data.com.

Passmore, David. "Searching For Directory Services." *Business Communications Review* 26(7): 18.

Petrosky, Mary. "Directories in the Limelight." *Network World* 15(11) 1.

Petrosky, Mary. "Get on Board the Directory Train." *Network World* 14(26): 43.

Web Articles

Anonymous "LAN Telephony: An Overview of Market Drivers, Applications, and Technology." www.3com.com/technology/research/topics/lan_telephony.html.

Chadwick, D. W. "Understanding X.500–The Directory." www.salford.ac.uk/its024/Version.Web/Contents.htm.

Goodman, David and Colin Robbins. "Understanding LDAP and X.500." Version 2.0, August 1997: www.eema.org/understanding_ldap.html.

Index

2884 84